KT-556-123

The FA

LEARNING

The Official FA Guide to
Running a Club

Les Howie

Hodder & Stoughton
A MEMBER OF THE HODDER HEADLINE GROUP

For order enquiries: please contact Bookpoint Ltd, 130 Milton Park, Abingdon, Oxon
OX14 4SB. Telephone: +44 (0) 1235 827720. Fax: +44 (0) 1235 400454. Lines are open
from 09.00–18.00, Monday to Saturday with a 24-hour message-answering service.
Details about our titles and how to order are available at www.madaboutbooks.com

British Library Cataloguing in Publication Data:
a catalogue record for this title is available from the British Library.

ISBN 0 340 816058

First Published 2004
Impression number   10 9 8 7 6 5 4 3 2 1
Year   2007 2006 2005 2004

Copyright © 2004 FA Learning Ltd

Managing Editor: Jonathan Wilson, FA Learning

Typeset by Servis Filmsetting Ltd, Manchester.
Printed in Great Britain for Hodder & Stoughton Educational, a division of Hodder
Headline Plc, 338 Euston Road, London NW1 3BH by Cox & Wyman, Reading, Berkshire.

Hodder Headline's policy is to use papers that are natural, renewable and recyclable
products and made from wood grown in sustainable forests. The logging and
manufacturing processes are expected to conform to the environmental regulations of the
country of origin.

Contents

LEARNING

Dedication

I would like to dedicate this book to three people who had a major influence on my development and career in running clubs, coaching and management:

David Beardall, the Wallsend Boys Club leader, who encouraged me to take responsibility and supported me when I ran my first league.

Peter Kirkley who took the 'risk' of allowing an enthusiastic 16 year old to become a coach, and who over the years has been a constant source of advice and encouragement.

Maurice Youdell who helped shape my professional development, by providing opportunities, challenges and support. Without these three people, I wouldn't be where I am today.

Thank you.

Philosophy of the guides

The aim of these **Official FA Guides** is to reach the millions of people who participate in football or who are involved in the game in other ways – at any level.

Each book aims to increase your awareness and understanding of association football and in this understanding to enhance, increase, improve and extend your involvement in the world's greatest game.

These books are designed to be interactive and encourage you to apply what you read and to help you to translate this knowledge into practical skills and ability. Specific features occur throughout this book to assist this process:

■ Tasks will appear in this form and will make you think about what you have just learned and how you will apply it in a practical way.

Best Practice The Best Practice feature will give you an example of a good or ideal way of doing things – this could be on or off the pitch.

Quote | 'Quotes throughout will pass on useful knowledge or insight or encourage you to consider a certain aspect of your skills or responsibilities.'

Statistic

The statistics included will often surprise and will certainly increase your knowledge of the game.

Summary

- **The summaries at the end of each chapter will recap on its contents and help you to consolidate your knowledge and understanding.**

You can read this guide in any way you choose and prefer to do so – at home, on the pitch, in its entirety, or to dip in for particular advice. Whatever way you use it, we hope it increases your ability, your knowledge, your involvement, and most importantly your enjoyment and passion to **be a part of the game**.

Introduction

Everyone has heard of the great international football clubs – the type that have fantastic stadiums, huge fan bases and superstar players throughout the squad such as Manchester United, Arsenal, Real Madrid, Juventus, Santos and Boca Juniors. Many football fans will also be aware of the smaller, less glamorous professional clubs in their own countries such as Mansfield Town and Hartlepool in England, Salamanca in Spain and Como in Italy.

But what about the hundreds of thousands of grassroots amateur clubs that play organized football in the thousands of local leagues and cup competitions throughout the world? In England alone there are over 35,000 affiliated clubs (members or registered clubs with The Football Association (The FA) or County FA).

The vast majority of these clubs provide recreational football for millions of players every weekend. They are run by volunteers who have a passion for the game and, without such dedication, grassroots football would not exist.

In this book, we will provide you with some practical advice and ideas about starting and running a local football club. We hope that you enjoy *Running a Club* and, most importantly, we hope that you are able to put some of the ideas into practice, and that they help you and your club.

Why start a club or run a team?

I am sure that this is a question everyone in football has asked themselves at some point, and detailed below are some of the reasons why people do start clubs and teams. In order for you understand why I am writing this book, I shall use myself as a case study.

My story

Like most young and not so young boys growing up in the North East of England in the 1970s, football was my passion. I was forever playing in the school playground, in the back lane and on the local playing fields. I was always trying to get into the school teams, and in my neighbourhood

I played at the local club, Wallsend Boys Club. In my spare time I enjoyed going with my dad to watch Newcastle United, and I have been lucky enough to see some of the club's greatest players such as Malcolm McDonald, Kevin Keegan through to Chris Waddle and Peter Beardsley.

I was an enthusiastic player but like most that take up the game, enthusiastic is as good as I got! At the age of 15 I realized that I was destined, if I was lucky, to be a Division 32 player in the local Sunday Leagues (and there's nothing wrong with that). However, two people who were involved in the running and administration of the local club, David Beardall and Peter Kirkley, encouraged me to try my hand at other aspects of the game.

Consequently, by the age of 15 I was refereeing and working as league secretary to the club's 16 teams in the five-a-side league. When I reached 16, I was encouraged and supported to take the next step and become the coach to the club's Under 11 team.

From that start, with encouragement and support, over the last 20 years I have held various positions in grassroots football. This has given me an opportunity to be involved in a great game and to make lots of friends. Yet wherever I've gone, I've always remembered the start, encouragement and support that were given to me.

Many people I come across in grassroots football tell me that they are involved because 'it's their club, and they want to put something back'. Others tell me they started their club so they could get a game! For some, it is a group of friends coming together, and for others it is about ensuring their children can play, so they get involved and run a youth team. Alternatively, people want to become part of their local community and to make friends. There are many reasons to join in, and the vast majority are positive.

At times you may become frustrated and irritated with the game, but I can honestly say that in all these years, I have met hundreds of like-minded, enthusiastic people who are passionate, and who gain and provide many, many hours of fun and purposeful activity.

The FA

LEARNING

Chapter 1

How to get started

THIS CHAPTER WILL:
- Explore what is needed to get you started.
- Describe the structure of football in England.
- Provide tasks that will help you to prepare and get your club off to a good start.

We appreciate that throughout the world the process for affiliation/registering clubs will differ and that different countries will have different names for their associations, local organizations and registration process. However, in an attempt to provide a useful guide for all readers, we have used the structure of English football as the case study for registering your club. In doing so, this chapter highlights many of the key issues and questions involved when a club is first started, wherever in the world you may be.

The structure

A good working knowledge of the structure of the game of football is important and avoids misunderstandings concerning the roles of the various organizations. The game of Association Football in England is organized, controlled, developed and governed by The Football Association (FA). It is played under the Laws of Association Football, which are controlled by The Fédération Internationale de Football Association (FIFA) and the International Football Association Board. The rules and regulations of The FA detail the manner in which football is controlled and administered throughout the country. The object of the rules and regulations is to enable the game to be governed throughout the country in a uniform manner.

Statistic

The FA was the world's first football association and was formed in **1863**.

County Football Associations

There are 43 geographical County Football Associations (County FAs) in England, as well as the Football Associations of The Amateur Football Alliance, The Armed Forces and the Islands of Guernsey, Jersey and the

Isle of Man, each of which is affiliated to The FA. The organization and control of the game played in each county is vested in the council of each County FA, and members of the council are able to help any league, club or individual with any problem that may arise. The work of each association is carried out by employees, committees and boards, who are responsible to each council.

Statistic

The **43** County FAs administer football for over **4 million** participants in England.

Leagues and clubs

Once a club is accepted into the membership of a County FA, it is required to abide by the rules of The FA, league or competition, and may be fined and/or otherwise disciplined if it breaches these rules. It is important to appreciate that in most cases, league officials are honorary officers and that a poorly-run club causes a great deal of additional work for all concerned. A club secretary, in particular, must have a good working knowledge of the rules of all organizations of which the club is a member. In the most serious cases of maladministration, a club may be expelled from its league, or where breaches of The FA or County FA rules have occurred, its affiliation may be suspended or withdrawn.

The first step

Quote | 'The first step is the hardest!'

As we said in the Introduction, the vast majority of football is played at a local level for personal enjoyment. Before embarking on forming a new team, the following two questions should be asked:

1 Are there enough potential players?
2 Are there enough volunteers to take care of club organization and administration?

Details of the major matters that you need to be aware of when setting up a club are covered below. However, if you need further information contact your County FA for assistance.

Affiliation

All clubs should affiliate to their respective County FA. It is through affiliation that the family of football is brought together, and correct standards and discipline are maintained. Affiliation acts as a quality assurance and safety net to help protect players, clubs, officials and administrators throughout the game. The major benefits from affiliation to your County FA include:

- Being part of the structure of the national game from grassroots upwards.
- Eligibility to participate in County FA competitions.
- Discipline and fair play.
- Opportunities to apply for grant aid and funding from The FA.
- Access to information and advice from:
  - County FA personnel.
  - FA Regional Football Development Managers.
  - FA Regional Facility Managers.
- Opportunities to acquire suitable public liability and personal injury insurance cover for your club, team and players.
- Access to FA and County FA publications and resources.
- Opportunities to participate in FA football development schemes.
- The chance to make your club's views on the future development of the game known to both your County FA and The FA.

Constitution: appointment of club officials

The club should have a constitution or code of rules. These are put in place to help the club operate. It is recommended that clubs should appoint a chairperson, treasurer and secretary to enable the club to function effectively within The FA's rules and regulations. Try to avoid press-ganging someone who does not want the responsibility, and remember that family members of players may be interested in the posts (see Chapter 7). It is also advisable to produce a list of the costs of running your team throughout the season, which will help you to create a budget of income and expenditure for the season (see Chapter 4).

Best Practice Always ensure that you have enough people willing to help and become involved in the club. Do not try to do everything yourself – you will need the support of those around you to take on the many responsibilities that are involved in running a club and making it sustainable.

Players: registration, eligibility, discipline and child protection

It is important that clubs are fully conversant with the rules of every competition that they may wish to enter. The County FA administers all discipline at grassroots level, and the secretary of the club is responsible for ensuring that all players are eligible to play. If the clubs have any doubts about eligibility, for example, suspensions, they should contact their County FA for details. For youth teams, it is important to observe The FA child protection policy, practices and procedures. An official of the club should attend an FA 'Child Protection and Best Practice' workshop.

■   Find out more about The FA's child protection policies by visiting **www.TheFA.com**.

Insurance: public liability, personal injury and other policies

Clubs are urged to obtain adequate insurance cover for their players in case of injury or accident while playing or travelling to matches. Please note this may be mandatory for some competitions or County FAs.

Clubs must also protect themselves by obtaining suitable public liability insurance. As the issues surrounding insurance can be complicated, we would advise that you contact your County FA to discuss any questions or concerns that you may have regarding insuring your club and players.

Quote | 'Think of the club and its players as you would your house and its contents. Would you ever consider not insuring your most treasured belongings?'

League membership

You have affiliated to your County FA and the appropriate league you wish to join, who must also be affiliated to the County FA. It is the role of the league to arrange fixtures for the teams and so, without affiliation to a league, the club could only play in friendly matches. If you are not sure which league your team should join or how to go about joining a league, you should seek advice on suitable league membership from the County FA. The easiest way to find out which leagues would be most suitable is to contact the County FA directly.

Which league to apply to for membership

Application for membership to a league or other competition must be made as early as possible in the year. Most leagues begin to formulate their divisions for the following season during April and May, and it is suggested that a new club makes initial contact with the league or other competition of its choice during February or March. New clubs could be disappointed if they leave their application any later than this. The most important consideration before applying is to establish which day the club wishes to play football (i.e. Saturdays, Sundays or mid-week).

▦   Find out from your County FA or local association about the most appropriate league for your team or teams to play in.

Club name

The name selected should be one that is unique to the individual club. County FAs will not permit a club to use the same or a similar name as one already affiliated because this may lead to confusion. To improve your chances of not having to pick a second name, try and research your local teams and come up with something original or, if in doubt, contact the local County FA.

Quote | 'Make sure you have confirmed your club name and checked that it is original before you get the kit made at the local supplier as it could be an expensive mistake!'

Pitches: useful contacts and advice

You should apply to the relevant Local Authority, Parish Council or private ground to hire a ground for matches. If you are not sure how to contact the relevant organizations, your local County FA should have their details, but the best alternative is to do some research in your local area. Please note that pitch hire charges will often vary greatly and you must take great care about terms and conditions of hire.

Best Practice   A good way to ensure that your club plays at the most suitable and well-equipped facilities is to drive around the local area, visit some pitches, speak to the individuals in charge, and talk to other managers about costs, service provided and availability.

Finance, fund-raising and bank accounts

As a new club, it is important to raise funds quickly to cover the essential expenditure such as affiliation fees, league membership fee, pitch hire charges (which often must be paid in advance) and kit. Decide the fee for members' annual subscriptions, and at which bank or building society to open an account in the club name. Make sure that signatories of the account keep the members fully informed, through the treasurer, of any expenditure and how much is in the account.

Always remember that every member of a club is likely to be a joint owner of any assets of the club, but is also jointly liable for all or part of any debts. Clubs should therefore consider suitable insurance or seek advice from appropriate league, competition or County FA representatives. It is also important to make provision for dealing with any cash, kit or other assets if the club ceases to exist.

Statistic

It costs, on average, **£2,500–£3,000** a season to run an adult club in England. However, over **50** weeks and with **15** members this is **£4** per week for each member – a lot less than the price of a game of golf!

Other items

Some of the other key items that require attention include:

- Club colours: you will need to decide what colour you want your club to play in, and you will need a contingency in case you play against a side with the same colours. As kits can be an expensive acquisition for the club, it is often difficult to pay for a second kit so make sure that you have at least some different coloured bibs in case this situation arises.

- Training facilities: training is obviously an essential element for any club, so make sure you do your research and look into potential facilities, their availability and costs.

- Match fees: how much the league charges the teams to play and how this impacts what you charge the players is an essential element that needs to be planned. When affiliating to a league, check the match fees.

The England team in training

• Annual general meeting: once the aforementioned items have
  been decided, the club's rules can be drawn up for adoption at
  the first annual general meeting (AGM). It is advisable to
  arrange for this meeting to be held in May or June. A copy of
  suggested standard club rules can be found in Appendix 1,
  p. 139.

Kit and equipment

You must make sure that you purchase suitable equipment prior to the
start of the season, and ensure you have sufficient equipment for all the
teams in your club. The necessary equipment will include playing strip,
first aid kit, nets, balls and cones. If you are unsure where to purchase
this equipment, contact the league or County FA – in many cases these
organizations will have deals in place to ensure that their clubs receive a
discounted rate.

■ Research the local suppliers and compare prices to make sure that your club is getting the best deal on its kit and equipment.

Administration

Look at the club action timetable (see Table 5, p. 31), which covers pre-season tasks both prior to and on the day of the game, discipline and the club AGM.

Results

Make sure that you comply with competition regulations by passing on the results of your matches to those responsible at either the leagues or County FA (depending on the match and competition). This helps with administration, and also allows results to appear in the local media or on the internet (if the league has a website).

Quote | 'Players will always be interested to see the results of their rivals and the latest league table, so make sure you get your results in on time and tell your players where they can find this information.'

Best Practice If you can, try to get your club online and design a simple website. This can be used to display latest results, league tables and fixtures, and to communicate directly with the players and volunteers.

Constitution/standard code of rules

Even the smallest clubs need rules to provide guidance for the better running of the club. Rules not only help in disputes, but often stop disputes from happening in the first place. If you are applying for any grants to start your club, you will be expected to have a constitution (a set of rules).

- Given the natural eagerness to form a club and to play matches, the next step is to persuade a keen and responsible person to ensure that FA regulations are conformed to.
- Club rules must be drawn up, affiliation to the County FA must be arranged, and membership must be organized to include a subscription, however nominal it may be.
- No County FA wants to reject or overrule initial keenness and information to help embryo clubs is sent out regularly.

Some years ago The FA, in response to many requests, drew up a list of suggested rules for newly formed clubs. This is of help to clubs worldwide. For suggestions of how to structure and present club rules, see Appendix 1 (p. 139).

Club policies

As your club develops, it may be appropriate to establish policies on anti-discrimination, equal opportunities, and a complaints procedure. Again, many sponsors and those offering financial assistance will expect any clubs or organizations they fund to be able to provide such policies.

As the governing body of the game in England, The FA is responsible for setting standards and values to apply throughout the game at every level, and The FA expects its clubs to set an example and establish good practice.

Football belongs to, and should be enjoyed by, everyone equally. The FA's commitment is to eliminate discrimination whether by reason of gender, sexual orientation, race, nationality, ethnic origin, colour, religion or ability, and to encourage equal opportunities.

Policies on anti-discrimination and equal opportunities can be found in Appendices 2 and 3 respectively (pp. 145 and 147).

Club complaints procedure

In the event that any member feels that he or she has suffered discrimination in any way or that the club policies, rules or Code of Conduct have been broken, they should follow the procedures below:

- Report the matter to the club secretary or another member of the committee. The report should include:

  - Details of what, when and where the occurrence took place.

  - Any witness statements and names.

  - Names of any others who have been treated in a similar way.

  - Details of any former complaints made about the incident, date, and when and to who they were made.

  - A preference for a solution to the incident.

- The club's management committee will sit for any hearings that are requested. This committee will have the power to warn about future conduct and suspend or remove from membership any person found to have broken the club's policies or Codes of Conduct. See the Code of Conduct in Appendix 6 (p. 154).

▓ Use the information above to design a club complaints procedure template.

Keeping records

It is important to have a record of your members and players so that you have all of their details to hand, as well as information such as contact details, medical conditions and parental consent. Appendix 4 (p. 149) gives an example of a membership registration form that you may wish to use or adapt.

Club meetings

It is also important that you keep a record of decisions made at committee meetings. These meetings do not have to be too formal, they could be as simple as a quick get-together over a drink, but without a record of what's agreed and who's responsible, at some stage, something important may be forgotten.

Below are some example agendas, for club meetings and your AGM, as well as a template to assist in recording decisions.

Club meeting agenda/AGM agenda

Club meeting agenda

- Apologies.
- Action points from last meeting.
- Financial matters.
- Team matters.

- Special events.
- Any other business.

Club AGM agenda

- Apologies.
- Notes from last AGM.
- Chairperson's report.
- Secretary's report.
- Annual accounts.
- Elections:
  - Chairperson.
  - Vice-chairperson.
  - Secretary.
  - Treasurer.
  - Committee.
- Any other business.

Table 1 **Club meeting minutes template**

Club:	**Date of meeting:**	
Present:		
Apologies:		
Action points:		
Action	**Responsible**	**Timescale**
Date of next meeting:		

Summary

- Know the structure and which County FA you should contact.

- Decide which league you wish to join.

- Establish your constitution and decide on the rules.

- Ensure that you register your players, and are aware of competition rules.

- Don't forget your club insurance.

- Book your pitch.

- Make sure you have the right kit and equipment in place.

- If you have rules and/or policies, work to them!

- Keep a record of players/members and meetings.

Self testers

1 What equipment do you need to get your club started?

2 Why affiliate to a league?

3 Who owns the assets of your club?

Action plan

I would like to find out more   Highlight all the questions that you may have as a result of reading this chapter and contact your local County FA so that it can give you answers or point you in the right direction.

Chapter 2

Who can help?

> THIS CHAPTER WILL:
> - Suggest who you can contact for help.
> - Explain what type of advice or help you are likely to receive.

In reality, every club will need help at some stage. Again, here we have used the structure of English football to detail who will be able to help you and your club. However, this information is easily transferable wherever you are, and similar systems and associations from which to gain support and help can be found in countries outside England.

County Football Association

As we have already covered in Chapter 1, there are 43 County FAs and you will find a team of professional staff in each, who will be only too pleased to provide help and advice.

County secretary/chief executive

This person will be a very experienced football administrator, who will be able to provide advice on the aspects of administration, for example:

- What forms you need to complete.
- Where to find the most appropriate leagues.
- Providing a set of the County FA's rules.

░ Find out the details of your county secretary or relevant football administrator, so that you have these to hand whenever the above questions arise.

Football Development Team

Every County FA has a Football Development Team – in the small counties this could be one person, while in some of the larger ones it is a team of five to six people. The development team will be able to provide advice on the courses listed below.

Football administration

This contains various elements that will provide you with practical advice on running your club. Topics covered include the development of your club, volunteer development, and how to market your club more effectively. Courses are usually available throughout the football season.

Coaching courses

County FAs usually provide three levels of FA Coaching Awards detailed in Table 2 opposite.

The County FA also offers medical courses and 'Child Protection' and 'Best Practice' workshops. The FA is continually developing training courses to meet the needs of those involved in football. To keep up to date, it is worth visiting The FA learning website at **www.TheFA.com/** falearning.

The FA has also developed an 'Introduction to Coaching Adults' course. This course, which lasts ten hours, provides practical advice and coaching tips. It includes resource books and a coaching video.

Table 2 **Coaching awards**

Course	For whom	Prerequisites	Where	What
Coaching Level 1	Coaches of young players	Open entry course for anybody over 16 years of age. You don't need to have any experience, just an interest in the game and motivation to improve your knowledge.	Locally run courses managed by County FAs that also take place residentially at approved FA centres.	Introduction to coaching, lots of practical ideas, includes child protection and emergency aid.
Coaching Level 2	Coaches with some previous experience at any level with regular participation.	Open entry course for anybody over 16 years of age with regular practical experience of participation in football.	Locally run courses managed by County FAs that also take place residentially at approved FA centres.	This course moves on to more technical aspects of the game.
Coaching Level 3	Coaches that are working with a team over an extensive period.	Anybody over 18 years of age. Candidates must hold the Level 2 certificate in coaching football.	Locally run courses managed by County FAs that also take place residentially at approved FA centres.	Moving on to coaching sides, match analysis, and the more advanced aspects of the game.
Coaching adults	Coaches in grassroots adult football	Open entry course	Locally run courses	Introduction to running an adult club, ideas on administering your club, and lots of practical coaching tips.

Club development

The FA has developed a Kitemarking scheme for grassroots clubs called Charter Standard. The aim of the scheme is to reward progressive forward-thinking clubs that place a high importance on club development and that meet The FA's criteria. Figure 1 and Table 3 opposite detail the structure of the Charter Standard scheme. This programme is about required standards and reaching excellence. In Chapter 8, we look at club development plans in more detail.

Funding opportunities

The development team staff will be able to provide advice on funding opportunities, for example:

- **The Football Foundation.**
- **Awards for All.**

Aside from your County FA, there are others who can also help you, and these are detailed on p. 24.

Figure 1 **The structure of Charter Standard**

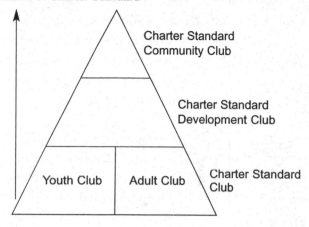

Table 3 **Charter standard**

Award	Basic criteria
Charter Standard Club	• Level 1 coach with every team. • Child protection trained staff. • Emergency aid qualified with every team. • Insurance. • Code of Conduct. • Constitution.
Charter Standard Adult Club	• Emergency aid qualified with every team. • Insurance. • Code of Conduct. • Constitution.
Charter Standard Development Club	Same as Charter Standard Club plus: • At least one Level 2 coach. • Minimum five teams. • Football development plan.
Charter Standard Community Club	Same as Charter Standard and Charter Standard Development Club plus: • Ten teams from mini-soccer to adult. • At least one male or female team. • Comprehensive development plan. • Volunteer co-ordinator.

League officials

Most league officials are volunteers like yourself, with years of experience, so don't be afraid to use them. If you have a question or query (especially when first starting out), in nearly all cases it will have been asked countless times before so make sure that you utilize all the contacts you make when registering your club.

Quote | 'League officials will be more than happy to give you advice. Remember that they will want to help you so always ask rather than keeping quiet if you are unsure about anything.'

Other clubs

Other clubs are often a great source of advice. Even if they are your fiercest rivals, remember that they are volunteers too and probably in the game for similar reasons to yourself. Would you give advice if asked by another club? The family of football needs to support each other, and if you are unsure talk to other managers and coaches.

Best Practice If you meet a really progressive club, such as a Charter Standard Club, arrange to meet them, ask them what they do and draw on their experience. You might be in competition on the pitch, but off it, you should work together for the good of the game.

Local Authorities

Main points of contact are:

1 **Pitch hire:** You need a pitch, and local councils are located in most parts of the country and are the main providers – find out who to contact, and get in early.

2 **Sports Development Team:** The Sports Development staff from your local authority will be able to provide advice on courses and possible local funding opportunities.

3 **Schools:** Two main advantages in linking to your local schools are:

   a If you're running a youth team, this is the best place from which to recruit your players.

   b Many schools have facilities that they rent out for training and for games.

▓ Some schools have Specialist Sports College status and, as part of this, they are encouraged to forge links with local sports clubs. In order to make the most of this, do some research and find out if there are any in your local area.

| Quote | 'When I was running a team I found that, over the years, I built up a contacts book of people and organizations which could provide help or advice. Do the same – it will become an invaluable resource to you.' |

To help you start your own list of contacts, complete Table 4.

Table 4 **Contacts list**

	Name	Telephone	E-mail
County FA secretary			
Development team			
League			
Local club			
Sports development team			
Pitch hire			
Local school			
Youth club			

Remember that this is just the beginning – keep this and continue adding to it.

Summary

- **Decide what you need help with.**

- **Develop contacts.**

- **Don't be afraid to ask for help.**

- **Remember to say thank you!**

- **Don't forget that one day someone will be asking for your help.**

Self testers

1 Who is the advised point of contact regarding completion of registration forms?
2 What is the name of The FA's club Kitemarking scheme?
3 Why would you contact a Local Authority?

Action plan

I would like more detail on the Charter Standard Scheme Carry out some research into The FA's Charter Standard scheme and, if outside England, investigate similar schemes in your local area.

Chapter 3

Administration of the club

THIS CHAPTER WILL:
- Look at how to keep the club running smoothly, throughout the year.
- Mid-season procedures.
- End of season procedures.

Club officials

The business and affairs of a club are generally managed and conducted by a committee consisting of the officers, the managers of the various teams and a number of ordinary members (usually players or supporters).

The officers of the club are normally a chairperson, vice-chairperson, honorary secretary, and honorary treasurer. In addition to these positions, a club may also have additional officers (e.g. a fixtures secretary, assistant secretary, press officer, social organizer). Officers are usually elected at the AGM, and hold office until the next AGM. Ordinary committee members are also elected at the AGM. Committee meetings are generally held on a monthly basis to deal with club business. The committee is responsible for the control of the club and the pursuance of its objectives as stated within the rules of the club. Club officers are also responsible for the day-to-day operation of the club within their specific areas of responsibility. All officers should be required to give a report at each committee meeting. In this way, the committee can keep proper control of the club's activities.

One person should not try to fill more than one of these functions because teamwork in the organization of a club is as essential as teamwork on the field of play.

| Quote | 'Remember that as your club progresses up the leagues, a greater number of duties/responsibilities may have to be undertaken by the club, and additional officers may be required (e.g. someone to produce a match day programme or a specialist fixtures secretary).' |

Chapter 7 looks at the roles of the volunteer and what each person is expected to do.

In the table opposite we have highlighted the key administrative tasks that will need to be performed by any new clubs in the form of a checklist so that clubs can make sure that everything that needs to be completed for the new season has been achieved and ticked off the list.

Mid-season procedures

Meetings that occur during the season

Many leagues/competitions have regular meetings throughout the season. These are good opportunities to stay in touch with other clubs and keep up to date with changes on relevant football developments.

Table 5 **Club action timetable/checklist**

Pre-season	Achieved	Comments
Players: Ensure that each team has a squad of at least 14 players or the appropriate number for mini-soccer/small-sided teams.		
Affiliation: Complete and forward appropriate documentation and fees to your County FA, league or other competitions.		
Facilities: Arrange pitch(es) that comply with appropriate league regulations and specifications. It is also prudent to arrange/book training facilities early.		
Risk assessment: Carry out a risk assessment on training and the playing venue (see Chapter 9).		
Meetings: Organize club/team meetings (e.g. weekly training, monthly management meeting, AGM). Also attend relevant league or County FA meetings when required.		
Registration: Make sure all players are registered with appropriate league and/or County Associations. Up-to-date photographs may be required.		
Friendly fixtures: Arrange fixtures with affiliated club secretaries.		
Subscription: Set a subscription for players and members to meet your costs for the season. Carry out fund-raising (appropriate to the club).		
Code of Conduct: As a club, agree a Code of Conduct for officials, players and spectators.		
Parents' night: If you have a youth section, organize a parents' night and distribute a club introductory pack (visit the Soccer Parent website: http://soccerparents.thefa.com).		

Club committee meetings

Your own club committee should meet to ensure that the club is running smoothly. A record of these meetings should be kept – this does not need to be complicated, just a record of any decisions or actions agreed (see the meeting template, Table 1, p. 15).

Players'/parents' meetings

These can be very informal, but are a great way to keep everyone in touch with your club, and they can be done as part of training.

Training

Does your club want to train? If yes, book your venue and set your coaching programme.

You may wish to make a copy of the following pages, to assist you throughout the season.

Table 6 **Home games checklist**

Date: _____

Kick off: _____

Fixture: _____ vs _____

Task	Achieved	Comments
Book/confirm pitch.		
Confirm to opposition team: • Kick-off time. • Directions. • Team colours.		
Confirm with match officials: • Kick-off time. • Venue and directions.		
Confirm kick-off time with your own team.		
On match day: • Ensure pitch is safe. • Ensure goalposts are secure (see 'Goalpost safety guidelines' on p. 128. • Are the goal nets up and corner flags in place? • Are the changing rooms open (and tidy)? • Pay the match officials. • Ensure all equipment is safely put away. • You may wish to provide refreshments.		

Table 7 **Away games (ideally six days prior) checklist**

Task	Achieved	Comments
Confirm with opposition team: • Kick-off time. • Directions. • Team colours. Confirm with your own players: • Kick-off time. • Venue. • Directions.		

Best Practice When you travel to away fixtures, always allow plenty of time in case there are any delays or problems on the way. Make sure that you have contact details of the opposing team just in case!

Be aware that for home and away games, the league/competition may require you to provide the referee with a teamsheet; this is a form that details all the players in the team.

Results

Complete the result card and post it to the appropriate league official to arrive by the designated time. Please note that the competition may require the result to be confirmed by telephone to the appropriate official. The level of detail on the result card (e.g. players, goal scorers, substitutions, injuries) will depend on league policy.

Starting a club allows you to become one of over 40,000 grassroots teams playing each week.

All coaches should be aware of The FA's policy on child protection.

Make sure your club has all the right kit. This includes the appropriately sized balls, goals and playing kit.

Make sure your club has alternative pitches to play on if yours becomes unavailable!

Make sure you are aware of the rules on age limits for mixed football.

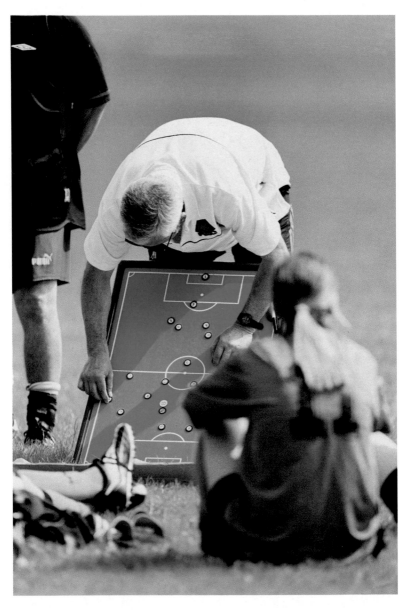

To maximize the potential of your players, support coaches to become
qualified whenever possible.

Best Practice Always check that your result card is correctly completed because this saves everyone's time.

Other tasks

Administration

Keep on top of your administration. Reply to correspondence promptly because this not only helps you, but also helps the other club or league officials who are also volunteers.

Disciplinary procedures

Unfortunately this is an ongoing task throughout the season. Remember that the more you can do to get players to stay out of trouble, the easier your job is. The secretary and player must complete and return appropriate documentation with fines. A record should be kept of players' discipline and any suspended players should not play.

Statistic

The FA conducts **140** disciplinary hearings each year, handling up to **10** cases at a time.

End of season procedures

AGM

As mentioned in Chapter 1 your club should hold an AGM to review the year, elect club officers and approve club accounts, but remember to set the date and venue and to notify members.

Accounts

The AGM should agree the annual accounts (see Chapter 4). Many County FAs ask for a copy of these accounts so remember to get accounts copied.

Presentation evening

It is good to have a presentation evening, not only for the players but to thank all the volunteers who keep the club going throughout the year. These are always good fun and it often makes a pleasant change to see players and volunteers in a social setting.

Quote | 'If run properly, events such as presentation evenings can be great ways to raise additional funds for the club.'

Other issues to consider

Referee matters

Appointments

Ensure that you know who is appointing the referees for the competitions your club will play in (for example, the county or league). Also, if a game is called off, remember to notify the appointments secretary – it will give them the opportunity to re-allocate your referee to another game.

Becoming a referee and training courses

Courses will be organized on a regular basis. Remember – it is everyone's responsibility to encourage and support referees. You can refer to another book in this series, *The Official FA Guide to Refereeing*, for more information on becoming a referee and how to get started.

Club assistant referees

Some competitions will permit substitutes to act as a club assistant referee. This is a volunteer within the club who is responsible for performing the role of the assistant referee if there are no assistant referees provided by the County FA. However, it is desirable to obtain the services of a non-playing member to perform this task. Remember fines may be incurred for failing to provide a club assistant referee as it makes the referee's job more difficult.

Child protection

This is an important aspect of football throughout the world. In England, The FA is leading the way in child protection and has developed a range of policies that aim to promote best practice and protect all children that play the game. For more information, see Appendix 5 (p. 152).

Statistic

In England alone, there are some **4 million** children who play football.

Advertising on players' kit

As will occur in most countries, in England, The FA sets restrictions on the type and size of advertising that may be carried on the players' kit. Clubs should check the details of this.

■ Check the restrictions on shirt sponsorship with your County FA (or relevant association). Make sure you do this before investing in any kit.

Mixed football

This differs between countries, so do check the rules of your national association. In England, mixed football is only permitted up to and including Under 11 teams. Players, officials and referees must not take part in matches involving mixed teams of men and women. Clubs must not permit mixed matches to be played on their grounds.

Matches against foreign opposition – at home and abroad

Permission must be obtained from The FA to play matches against foreign opposition. Application forms are available from County FAs. For all such matches, please give as much notice as possible but in any event not less than 14 days because clearance has to be obtained from the

other national associations involved. This policy will differ worldwide, so again, please research the guidelines concerning this issue.

Small-sided football

Competitions

Small-sided football is increasing in popularity. This has been recognized in England and The FA has developed a specific set of rules regarding small-sided competitions. All tournaments, irrespective of the duration, the number of teams taking part or the number of players on each team, must be sanctioned by the local County FA. The competition organizer is required to complete and submit the appropriate forms to the relevant County FA.

Leagues

As above, you must make sure that the league in which you participate is properly sanctioned. In the case of small-side leagues, clubs must follow the same affiliation procedures as 11-a-side teams.

Field misconduct and discipline

Suspensions imposed for field offences apply to all forms of football. Players suspended after an offence in a small-side competition are also suspended from 11-a-side matches, and vice versa.

First aid equipment

Each club should provide a properly maintained first aid kit at all matches and should send members on FA 'Treatment of Injury' courses (or a relevant course). Information concerning the availability of such courses will be regularly communicated directly to clubs, and where this is not the case we would advise clubs to research this area. It is extremely important that every club should have at least one qualified member to attend to each team.

Best Practice So that your club has adequate basic first aid knowledge, make certain that, wherever possible, all members complete a first aid course.

International clearance

Many clubs ignore or are unaware of the fact that players who have recently played football in another national association may not play football in their chosen country without an International Transfer Certificate. Furthermore, this includes England players who have played in Scotland and Wales. Application for international clearance should be made directly to the relevant national association. In England, The FA does not charge for this service.

Matches or training on religious or spiritual festival days

Allowances must be made for national or religious festivals, and players and club officials must be considerate of their team mates' wishes. Players cannot be forced to play on the festival days of their particular

religion, for example, Good Friday, Christmas Day, Ramadan (Muslim month of fasting), Divali (Hindu and Sikh Festival of Light), Yom Kippur (Jewish Day of Atonement), Hanamatsuri (Japanese Buddhist flower festival), Passover (Jewish festival).

Travelling away

If your club organizes trips away for young people, the following section will provide practical advice.

Every year many young players travel away for training and matches. Sometimes these involve just a day trip; increasingly they involve longer excursions within the country or abroad. Inevitably, there are additional implications for best practice and for ensuring the safety and welfare of young players away from home.

When planning an event away from home or club, you need to consider these points:

- Has the club, organization or team fully implemented policies and procedures for ensuring the welfare of children in terms of the:
  - Recruitment of volunteers?
  - Reporting procedures?
  - Observance of the Code of Conduct?
- Where possible ensure that every member of the club staff involved in the trip has successfully completed the relevant child protection training, for example, The FA offers both a distance learning pack and a three-hour 'Best Practice' workshop.
- Has a risk assessment for the trip been conducted? No amount of planning can guarantee a safe and incident-free trip, but good planning and attention to safety measures can reduce the likelihood of serious incidents. Check travel, venue, staffing, weather/environment, sleeping and catering arrangements for potential hazards, and put safety and emergency procedures in place.

- Is there sufficient insurance cover? Consider:
  - Public liability including civil liability.
  - Personal accident which should include a no-fault pay out.
  - Travel insurance including necessary provision for accident, breakdown and recovery if you are using self-drive vehicles.
  - Medical cover including repatriation expenses.
- Are visas required? Do you need to consider any cultural factors (e.g. dos and don'ts), environmental conditions (e.g. heat, insects) or medical issues (e.g. malaria tablets, vaccinations)?
- What staffing is needed? The staff-to-player ratio will be determined by:
  - Risk assessment.
  - The age of players – 1:10 staff-to-player ratio is recommended for players over 11, more staff are recommended with younger children whether single or mixed sex. If mixed, there should be at least one male and one female.
  - Any special needs – more staff are needed if there are players with medical needs or disabilities.
- Have the roles and responsibilities been clarified? Who has ultimate responsibility? The coach often has ultimate responsibility, the team manager is normally responsible for supervision and the driver should not have other duties while travelling.
- Is there a club/home contact? This person should hold copies of itinerary, all players' home addresses, venue contacts, and medical and consent forms.
- Have ground rules for the players been drawn up? It will be necessary to agree some rules during travelling and at the venue, particularly where there is remote supervision (for example, on a shopping trip, after an event, during social activities). A credit-card sized 'safe away card' that can be carried by each player at all times is strongly recommended.

This should include details of where you are staying and an emergency contact number.

- What is the accommodation? Check on security arrangements, storage of valuables, policies on smoking/drinking, catering arrangements and access to TV channels.

- What are the sleeping arrangements? There should be separate sleeping, washing and toilet facilities for males and females, staff and players. Players should not share a bed and staff should not share rooms with players. Ensure that there is a member of staff on each floor of the accommodation, and try to avoid sharing accommodation areas with other people. What medical back-up is available at the venue? What emergency procedures are in place?

Best Practice When preparing for an away trip, make certain that the parents/carers of each child are informed of all the contact details and itinerary. Keep them up to date with any changes and, where possible, call the parents before the trip to make sure that they, and you, have all the information required.

In preparation for the away trip, remember to:

- Provide appropriate information for parents/carers in writing and, if possible, discuss at a face-to-face meeting. This might include travel arrangements, contact numbers, itinerary, medical information, discipline policies, consent forms, pocket money, phoning home arrangements, homesickness, remote supervision agreements, staff-to-player ratios, kit and equipment list, emergency arrangements, cost and insurance.

- Gain written parental consent. This should include acceptance of the Code of Conduct, any medical information, special requirements and consent for emergency treatment.

- Provide guidance for players. This could be done in part at the parents' briefing, but might also be used to draw up and agree codes of behaviour, support (e.g. designated person for welfare issues), supervision, rooming arrangements (may need to be assigned rather than chosen), roles and responsibilities.

Paperwork checklist:

- Travel tickets, passports and visas.
- Medical papers.
- Contract/booking forms.
- Parental and medical consent forms.
- Home contact numbers.
- Insurance documentation.
- Medical services and location details.
- Photographs of all players and staff for emergencies.

On arrival at the destination, always carry out the following:

- Check rooming arrangements and match with rooming list, check rooms and meal times.
- Arrange safe keeping of money and valuables.
- Draw up rooming and contact lists, including staff rooms.
- Hold a briefing meeting to clarify issues and hand out safe away cards.

During the time away, make sure you consider:

- The need for daily briefings to discuss the day's events, problems and future planning.
- The provision of an opportunity for players to speak with staff if required.
- Holding daily staff meetings to review, plan and troubleshoot.

Best Practice After the trip, it is advisable to convene a staff debriefing session to discuss what went well, what did not go well, what has been learnt, and to make recommendations for future trips.

Summary

- **Use the checklists provided to assist you.**

- **The more you plan and prepare, the easier the task becomes.**

- **Get into a routine.**

- **Remember that the simpler you make it, the easier it is!**

Self testers

1 What ratio of staff to players is recommended for trips abroad for children over 11?

2 What is the age limit for mixed football in England?

3 What are the three main types of meetings that occur during the season?

Action plan

Who could I ask in our club to help? Look at the volunteer network within your club and attempt to assign roles based on a person's abilities, interests and attributes.

Chapter 4

Managing finance

THIS CHAPTER WILL:
- Provide some practical advice to keep your club's finances on the straight and narrow.
- Look at the likely costs of running a club.
- Help your understanding of budgeting.

No matter what level of club you run, at some stage money will become an issue. Obviously the bigger the club, the more finance is an issue. You just have to read the sports pages with regular news of well-established clubs facing financial troubles to be aware of this.

Quote | 'However much fun being involved in football is, finance is also an essential part of the game without which clubs would be unable to continue. Make financial awareness a top priority to ensure the fun never stops!'

Financial requirements of a club

The role of treasurer

Even the smallest club will, during the year, have a considerable amount of money passing through its hands. The necessary acquisitions such as kit and footballs, as well as the affiliation and match fees that have to be paid, will usually come from a combination of the players' fees, fund-raising events and sponsorship. This all adds up to a considerable amount of income and expenditure which must be accounted for. Consequently, the role of treasurer is central to the running of the club. Table 8 opposite highlights the typical cost of running a football team in England, although this will differ depending on location, both nationally and internationally.

With money passing through the club, it is vital to appoint a club treasurer. Chapter 7 gives further information on the role and responsibilities of the treasurer.

Table 8 **Income and expenditure**

Income
- Sponsorship   £400.00
- Membership
  (20 × £5)   £100.00
- Player fees
  (20 × £3 × 40 wks)   £2,400.00

Total   **£2,900.00**

These figures are conservative based on one team.

Expenditure
- County FA affiliation/insurance   £100.00
- League fees   £100.00
- Referee fees
  (20 (home matches) × £15)   £300.00
- Pitch hire   £1,000.00
- Kit   £500.00
- Kit washed!
  (£7 × 40 games)   £280.00
- First aid   £100.00
- Balls   £150.00

Total   **£2,530.00**

Raising the money

Now you have an idea of how much you will need, you should think about how you will raise this income:

Sponsorship

Sponsorship can come in a variety of forms, and we would recommend that clubs think creatively about how to get sponsors involved. Most clubs will have a kit sponsor, but other opportunities should not be ignored.

■　Think about what items cost the club the most money, and see if you could get a sponsor to provide these requirements, for example, footballs and trophies.

Subscriptions

These are the fees that players pay to play in each match. Subscriptions need to cover the majority of costs, although the fee charged will depend on the other sources of income generated by the club.

Membership fee

Each player should be expected to contribute financially to the running of the team. It is the role of the treasurer to ensure that the fee paid is enough to assist the running of the team, however you must set the fees carefully so that players are happy to pay the amount required, and do not join another team where the fees are lower. Note that a membership fee is usually a one-off payment at the start of the year and subscriptions are weekly fees paid by those who participate.

Other sources of income

Clubs should look at different ways to raise cash, including:

- **Weekly raffles.**
- **Presentation evenings.**
- **Sponsored events.**
- **Race/casino nights.**

Having done all this, do you have a deficit or a surplus income? If you have a surplus, then great, because during the season you will probably use it! If it is a deficit, you will need to raise your weekly subs or consider other ways to gain more funding.

Bank account

Every club should have a bank account in the name of the club. You should obtain monthly statements. Apart from an agreed amount of petty cash, all monies should be paid into the bank account.

The club should have a cheque book, but cheques must be signed by two agreed signatories. This is to protect everyone – club, individuals, and particularly the treasurer.

Best Practice Remember to keep a record of all income and expenditure. All items should be checked off against the monthly bank statements.

Petty cash

Agree as a club how much each team should be allowed to have as petty cash. A good working figure is about £50.00. Just as records are kept on the bank account, it is important that a petty cash record is kept.

Examples of financial accounting templates

These templates are used to track the total weekly costs which are often made up of numerous small payments that occur regularly.

Table 9 **Weekly club/team account sheet**

Club: _____

Team: _____

Item	Cost

To help the treasurer, you could use weekly account sheets, like Table 9 on the previous page. Each team could complete a sheet, and the treasurer could complete an overall club sheet.

Table 10 **Annual budget sheet**

Item of expense	Projected costs
Administration	
Equipment hire	
Equipment purchase	
Hire of facilities	
Officials' fees/expenses	
Promotion/Publicity	
Coaches' fees/expenses	
Session fees/expenses	
Transport	
Medals/trophies	
Total costs	

Income type	Projected income
Match day fees	
Membership fees	
Sponsorship	
Grants	
Other (e.g. raffles and presentation evenings)	
Total income	
Total profit/deficit	

Regular financial reports

At every committee meeting, the treasurer should present a financial update. This keeps everyone in the picture, and increases accountability.

Do not overstretch

Quote | 'If you haven't got the money, don't spend it!'

The new strip in the latest style may look good, and it might be a bargain at £1,200, but not if the club only has £300! Remember that as a club you are responsible for any bills and debt, so stick to the budget, or if you really like that kit, raise some more funds.

Community Amateur Sports Clubs

In England, clubs that provide amateur sporting activities (that is every football club that does not pay players) can register, through their local Inland Revenue office, to be a Community Amateur Sports Club (CASC). As a CASC registered club, you will be able to claim 28p for every pound that is donated to you. For example, if a player makes a donation over the year of £150 at £3 per week, you would be able to claim £42 back from the Inland Revenue under the CASC gift aid scheme.

■ Find out about registering for CASC by contacting your local Inland Revenue office or, if outside England, find out if there is a similar scheme that can help you.

Annual accounts

Every club should produce a set of annual accounts. These should show opening balance, income, expenditure and closing balance.

Summary

• **Set your budget, stick to it and don't overstretch.**

• **Keep records for the club's bank account and petty cash.**

• **Don't forget the importance of regular reports, and the need to produce annual accounts.**

Self testers

1 What factors do you need to take into account when deciding how much to charge players for match day fees?

2 What is the recommended amount of petty cash your club should have to hand?

3 Why should a regular update of the club's account be made available to members?

Action plan

How can we raise more funds?   Write a plan that highlights what you can do at your club to generate additional sources of income.

Chapter 5

Sponsorship and marketing: selling your club

> THIS CHAPTER WILL:
> - Explain the meaning of sponsorship for grassroots clubs.
> - Give hints on how to market your club.
> - Look at how to attract sponsors.

Quote | 'Good sponsorship requires more than just putting a sponsor's name on an event.'

Sponsorship is a two-way process – the sponsor takes something from your club; the club receives the sponsor's input and support. It can be complicated, but it is important to remember that successful sponsorship requires two parties to be happy about the relationship. Good sponsorship requires more than just putting a sponsor's name on an event.

Consumers need to be told about a sponsorship – and this is the responsibility of both parties. The sponsor should broadcast their involvement in local or regional press to gain maximum benefit, and the club should make sure that the sponsor is recognized for their input. Sponsorship gives the sponsor a degree of ownership over a new property that may have little to do with the sponsor's original business. In clubs that have a vibrant sponsorship programme, there will be various levels of sponsorship. For instance, a club sponsor will take precedence over an individual match sponsor, who will take precedence over the ball sponsor. Although this pecking order needs to be acknowledged, it is crucial that all sponsors are given the recognition they deserve. As the sponsorship market has evolved, expectations on both sides have changed completely. Sponsorship should no longer be seen as a means of covering the cost of an activity: it has become a vital part of football's promotion and development.

Football is a big business. As the world's most popular game, football has a unique reach throughout all age groups and sexes, and across more countries than any other sport in the world. This popularity and range means that any level of football is important to potential sponsors, from the World Cup to Sunday football in local parks.

Statistic

At the very top of the sponsorship pyramid, the last World Cup attracted television audiences measured in billions, and company sponsorship of around **£25 million** from each company.

The companies that sponsor the World Cup pay such huge amounts because of what the sponsorship enables them to do beyond the games themselves, and not just for the perimeter boards. While a Sunday morning game played in mud and rain is far removed from this, it is still part of the world of football and allows sponsors to be part of the world's most popular sport.

Quote | 'Sponsorship is a form of communication with staff, customers and the media, and at the highest levels with shareholders and opinion formers.'

Sponsors can be extremely varied in their size and financial input, but they all share some characteristics which bring them to football. Sponsorship is a form of communication, both internally within a company, and externally to customers and the media. Commercially, companies use sponsorship to improve the image of their products or services, to associate themselves publicly with the positive attributes of the sponsored sport or club, to reach more potential customers, and to create a feeling of giving something back into the local community. This rule is the same for Umbro as for the local butcher!

Ultimately, a sponsor wants publicity – anyone who is prepared to invest money without recognition is better described as a benefactor. This publicity can take many different forms, but all football sponsors want their enterprise to be connected positively with football. It is therefore important that football as a total entity grows and flourishes. For example, the success of the England team affects football at all levels in England – supporters, fans, players and children.

When sponsorship agreements are drawing to an end, it is likely that they will be re-evaluated and their media exposure will be a vital part in increasing value. If, over the period of the term, you have been able to demonstrate that the partnership with your club has proved to be successful in creating good positive exposure for the sponsor, this will help in negotiating a renewal of your agreement and an increase in the value of it.

To demonstrate this value, designate someone at the club to keep a record of local media coverage. Weekly clippings of fixtures and results would be repetitive, but team photographs, match reports, previews of cup competitions or important league matches, news about prizes won (for example, player of the match or raffle prizes), announcements of sponsorships, season previews and new signings would be valuable to keep a track of.

■   Think about who would be the best person at your club to keep a media record. Who always seems to know what's happening and knows whether your club has been mentioned in the local newspaper?

A list should be compiled and the boundaries of delivery (what the club could provide if a sponsor bought the rights to some or all of the club's properties) agreed. For example, a list might include some or all of the following properties your club will own that may provide sponsorship opportunities for your club: an advertising board at any football ground, a sponsor's sign in the clubhouse bar or a team photo in the local paper. These would all have a value in terms of the number of people who see them, and how much it would cost elsewhere to 'buy' similar space.

How to market your club

Every club will need to publicize its offering. Careful consideration needs to be given to possible sponsors when compiling a target list.

Sponsorship/Marketing committee

Prior to identifying the opportunities that your club has to offer to potential sponsors, it may be wise to create a sponsorship or marketing committee. This will help to form a collective view about what your club does or does not want to offer to potential sponsors.

The co-ordination and management of sponsorship and publicity requirements must be well disciplined. It makes sense for one individual to be appointed to manage all sponsorship, marketing, media relations and public relations (PR) activity, since they are all interrelated. If responsibilities are divided, a system needs to be put in place so that opportunities are maximized, sponsors rewarded, and activity positively co-ordinated.

Available club properties and rights

The next step is to identify and understand the 'properties' of your club that are available to sponsor. A list should be compiled, and the boundaries of delivery agreed. To illustrate, a list might include all or some of the following sponsorship opportunities:

- Club sponsors.
- Match programme (including advertising).
- Match tickets.
- Shirts sponsor (different sponsors for different teams is acceptable).
- Individual players.
- Signage (perimeter boards, clubhouse, stands, turnstiles, sponsor's recognition board).
- Match sponsor.
- Match ball sponsor.
- Player of the match.
- Food and drink provision.
- Club facilities (clubhouse).
- Awards (player of the year, young player of the year, top goal scorer, supporters' player of the year, club person of the year, volunteer of the year).
- End of season dinner.

Who is in the market?

Carefully consider possible sponsors and write a target list before any approaches are made. In this way, the best prospects are approached first, rather than following the temptation to approach the easiest first.

Think about some possible companies who you would prefer to sponsor your club and why. Is it because they have a good reputation, or because you think they have the financial capability to do so?

Listing major companies in the region

Even the largest companies are worth approaching since they may have community or recruitment issues that they can address through sponsorship. Some lateral thinking may be required to establish why a company might be interested in a sponsorship of your club, which might seem superficially too unimportant for it. However, remember that approaches at the highest level are never wasted – a company will remain aware of the opportunity in the future, and sponsorship is an ongoing process.

Large companies who might be worth considering include:

- A multinational company building a new facility.
- An established company extending its existing facility.
- An established company closing a facility elsewhere and concentrating on your region.
- A company with a poor local reputation.
- A company whose profits are growing.
- A company relocating employees.
- Any new company.
- Any company that advertises in national or local media.
- A company that supplies relevant services for football (from sportswear to lawnmowers).

Most of these companies will have websites and by using these you can usually assess the likely interest in sponsorship of your club. Look at the sponsorship, community affairs or charitable sections of the site to see if they are active in supporting similar community organizations to your club.

Listing local companies

Companies that only trade in the locality have even more reason to use sponsorship as part of their marketing since they are dependent on local people as employees, or for buying their goods or services. As before, it is sensible to compile a list of such companies before approaching any.

Best Practice Individuals within your club can provide a good starting point for creating lists of companies by using contacts, employees and their knowledge of local businesses.

Local companies can be grouped into a hierarchy ranging from companies with employees, down to sole traders. Individuals have historically played an important part in contributing to clubs, leagues and associations, but often their involvement has been one of benefactor rather than sponsor. In other words, they have effectively donated their money rather than sought a commercial return. True sponsorships should be presented so that business opportunities are opened up, benefits to the sponsor are clearly identified, and the value of the sponsorship increases accordingly.

Consider local companies who could also provide products or services in kind that your club would otherwise have to pay for (For example, kit, equipment, food, accountancy services). Local companies who might be worth contacting include:

- **Sports shops.**
- **Newsagents.**
- **Local grocers.**
- **Chemists.**
- **Insurers.**
- **Pubs.**
- **Car dealerships/Garages.**

There is no ideal length for your list, but it must be comprehensive. In a world of supply and demand there is no harm in generating multiple interests in a single property! A word of warning however, it is not a good use of valuable club members' time or resources to send a generic letter to a long list of companies that you have found quickly in the local Yellow Pages. It is much better to have 20 well-thought out and relevant organizations to approach.

How to attract sponsors

Quote | 'Attracting sponsors is all about presenting a positive image.'

Sponsorship is a competitive environment, and the opportunity your club has to offer must appeal to sponsors as a cost-efficient commercial enterprise. There may be a multitude of other clubs or organizations within your local community who are looking for similar levels of support, so the more you can stand out and present yourselves as more professional the better!

How to present and communicate

At the initial stage, the decision makers within a potential sponsor company may be completely ignorant of your property and its potential. It is vital that the first communication generates interest. This first contact will depend upon the size and scale of the sponsorship sought. Although some clubs may be looking for sponsorship of their properties, which run to thousands of pounds, many will be looking for support that is far less costly. Therefore, although investing time and money into the production of a small brochure might be right for some, for most clubs it is not appropriate. However, at the very least, a professional letter of introduction needs to be prepared which explains the opportunities your club is offering and why the selected company might be interested. This letter need not be a formal proposal, but should contain sufficient details about the opportunities and benefits to interest and tempt the potential sponsor, while making clear the likely cost to the sponsor.

▨ Draft a letter of introduction and ask other people in your club to read it and give you advice or suggestions on what to include. It is worth putting a lot of effort into this now because you will be able to use the same structure for any future introduction letters to companies.

Remember that the potential relationship is a 'partnership', and there should be flexibility on both sides to understand what both parties want to get out of it. The introduction letter should be tailored to individual companies and people, and should suggest a telephone call to ascertain interest in meeting to explore the benefits. That follow-up call should be made within two weeks of the letter's arrival. Responses will fall into one of three categories – interested, definitely not interested, or require further information. In the first case, a meeting should be arranged, and in the second, reasons for non-interest should be discovered if possible.

Best Practice It is important to find out why a company or person is not interested in sponsoring your club. It may be that they are financially unable to do so, or it could be something to do with your presentation of the possible sponsorship – you can learn from this, or may even be able to change decisions with this knowledge.

Once a meeting has been agreed, a more thorough preparation should be made. More background information on the prospective sponsor's business needs to be researched. In attracting sponsors to your club, it is important to present as many positive opportunities and reasons for involvement as possible. Even if half are thought unnecessary, one of the other suggestions might convince a prospective sponsor.

The file of clippings and media coverage will be useful in encouraging a prospective sponsor to imagine the benefits that sponsorship can bring.

People enjoy seeing their name in the media! Flexibility is also important – rather than presenting a fixed package of rights and benefits, it is useful to be able to accommodate potential sponsors' requests. However, exclusivity is crucial to sponsors. A sponsorship is dramatically weakened if the rights and benefits are shared with another similar business. For example, if a local pub has agreed to sponsor the first team at your club, they may not be happy if another pub in the community is allowed to sponsor your reserve team.

Agreeing delivery

Best Practice A written letter of agreement should be drawn up in case of future problems and to clearly state all details of the sponsorship.

Before signing any written agreement, both parties must be quite clear about their mutual responsibilities. Even at club level where the support may be financially less significant, there should be a letter outlining the agreement signed by the two parties. This not only clearly sets out the nature and specifics of the agreement for each party, it also communicates a level of professionalism on the part of your your club. Important elements within a written agreement include:

- Duration of the agreement.
- Renewal period.
- Fee to be paid and the timing of payment.
- What the club will do for the sponsor.
- What the sponsor will do for the club.
- Sponsor's logo or references and where they will appear.
- Limits to the sponsorship.
- Definition of contract breaking.

- Exit from contract.
- Rights and obligations.

How to value the sponsorship

Quote | 'As with houses, the value of sponsorship depends on what a sponsor is prepared to pay.'

To help evalute the sponsorship, suggestions have to be made and a valuation produced. The basic value will depend upon the publicity generated and again reference to a clippings file for local press coverage of your club will be very useful. When agreeing a sponsorship value, prices are likely to drop and an upper figure should be suggested as a starting point. Apart from the publicity value, there is a value connected to the status of a relationship with your club. If your club is well established and respected within the local community, it might achieve a higher valuation because of the local prestige it will bring to a sponsor. A third element in valuation are the exploitation opportunities, which may bring sponsors commercial reward. For example, if a local pub sponsors a team and agrees that the team will drink there after games, extra business will accrue, together with the opportunity for club functions to be held there, and other events such as end of season presentation nights. This would all be of incremental value to the sponsor and should be considered in the valuation of the sponsorship. It cannot be emphasized enough that for a sponsorship to work successfully, the sponsor should spend the same amount on promoting the sponsorship as on the sponsorship itself.

Although this may not apply for many clubs at grassroots level, it is undoubtedly true that sponsorships work better if they are publicized beyond the minimum level you have both agreed. It is worth discussing how much potential sponsors are prepared to promote the relationship with your club. For instance, the sponsor may agree to promote matches, awards nights or coaching courses at your club in their own shops or businesses. Finally, consider the costs in delivering the rights you have offered to sponsors. If you have agreed to guarantee your club sponsor some signage to go around the pitch or in the bar, find out what this is going to cost you to produce. This applies to everything you are planning to include in the agreement; the last thing you want is the menu of rights you are giving to a sponsor to cost you more to deliver than the sponsor is paying!

▦   Think about the things your club already has that could be sponsored. This does not have to be as simple as balls or kit – it could be the newsletter you produce or the weekly raffle.

How to deliver

From the sponsor's point of view, the delivery of these promised elements will be sufficient to justify their financial investment. Nevertheless, in addition to guaranteed delivery, it is sensible to seek ways in which the sponsor's expectations can be exceeded – without disproportionately increasing the cost of running the sponsorship.

Quote | 'Creating a personal involvement between the sponsor and your club can be very beneficial.'

A personal involvement between club and sponsor can be encouraged by:

- Inviting the sponsor as your guest to matches or events beyond their own sponsorship.
- Calling the sponsor after an event to check that all arrangements were satisfactory.
- Delivering a report at the end of a season, proving the value of the sponsor's investment.
- Discussing whether there are any new elements to the partnership that they wish to explore and making sure that they are happy in every respect.
- Making sure that if a sponsor is invited to an event, they are properly looked after and cared for – ignoring their well-being might have damaging effects.
- Treating the sponsor as a partner. The sponsorship of a property should not be seen as a one-off sale, but as a continuing relationship which can be improved to the benefit of both parties.
- Seeing the sponsor as a key supporter – one that is treated with courtesy and with respect to their interests.

How to promote and improve properties

Quote | 'Good publicity is much more valuable in a small publication than no mention elsewhere.'

Sponsorship is a continuing process and it is vital to try to improve sponsorship opportunities at your club. To illustrate, if your club has previously only received a fixtures and results service in the local press, but begins to attract photographs, match reports and other local coverage, both the event and the sponsor will benefit. It is beneficial for clubs to produce a short history of themselves, some interesting facts or a photograph and profile to issue as a press release at the start of a season.

Best Practice Know who your key contacts are in the local press. If you can, build up a relationship between themselves and the club, which will encourage them to give your club positive media coverage.

Knowing the key contacts in the local press is vital – if only to ensure your details are going to the right person. If you can, invite them to specific matches, festivals, presentations or coaching courses – it will not only educate them about what you and your sponsor are doing, but also it will hopefully repay itself in positive media coverage. The creation of positive news about your club – surprising results, record scores, record attendances, hat tricks, award winners, coaching courses – for release to local media will provide good stories. Moreover, it is not always necessary to have an upbeat story to promote – news items need not be about winning. The length of time a team has gone without winning or scoring is still newsworthy, especially when they do finally score! Most areas have both paid for and free local newspapers. If more senior teams dominate the area, it makes sense to create a special relationship with one of the smaller publications. Good publicity is much more valuable in a small publication than no mention elsewhere, and people will start to look out for your club news in that publication if it appears regularly.

Since sponsorship is an ongoing element of the game, improvements should always be considered. There may be risks involved in change, and bear in mind elements that might be lost through change since it is often difficult to recapture them. However, change can be seen in a positive light and can bring additional benefits. As well as internal suggestions, external suggestions should be listened to carefully and assessed – especially if they are made by a sponsor or by a potential sponsor. The best ideas will work towards mutual benefit – the worst will be one-sided.

■   If your club has sponsorship, assess its value and consider any things that could be changed to improve the partnership or that would be of benefit to the club and sponsor. Raise the best ideas you have at a committee meeting, or discuss them with other people involved in sponsorship at your club.

Future considerations

Quote | 'When considering renewal or the end of a contract, it is wise to review the value of the sponsorship.'

While time and effort are needed to ensure that existing sponsorship arrangements are implemented successfully, it is also necessary to think about future developments. Even if you have an excellent relationship with your club sponsors and you believe they will renew the following term, many factors prevent them from doing so and your club needs to plan accordingly. The last thing your club needs is to have budgeted for the following season based on income from sponsors, and have it taken away for reasons beyond their control (for example, a change in personnel or in the sponsor's business). Therefore, so that your club does not have to start again from the beginning, you need to discuss in advance with the sponsor their feelings about renewing.

You should also consider other sponsors who may be interested in your club who will, if nothing else, provide a good indication of the value of a sponsorship. In a situation where the existing sponsor is likely to renew, it is sensible to gain written agreement before the expiry of one contract or agreement – especially if an increase in fee is being proposed. The length of time required for this will vary, but a minimum of three months before the end of a season is recommended. When contemplating renewal or the end of a contract, it is wise to review the value of the sponsorship within your club's relevant committee to ensure that everyone is in agreement. It is likely that football will continue to be of interest to a very wide number of sponsors and to demonstrate the benefits and to build relationships – potential new sponsors can always be invited to matches or events.

There is no harm in increasing the desirability of a sponsorship during the contract of one sponsor – it is always safer to have a fallback, and new potential sponsors may be interested in different sponsorship opportunities. At the very least, the sponsorship will be newly marketed and knowledge of its worth increased. If a sponsorship is taken over by a new sponsor, it is very important to actively manage the changeover. First, understand and record why the initial sponsor is not renewing, and if an element needs to be corrected, do so. Second, in addition to any contract, learn the business requirements and expectations of the new sponsor.

It is a fact of life that people are different. A new sponsor may require a completely different approach to the previous one, and what worked in the past may not work in the future. New sponsors need to be treated exactly as such: they will not be interested in the successes or glories of the past, but in achievements in the future.

In conclusion, the following steps should be followed in this order:

1 **Appoint one individual to co-ordinate all of your club's sponsorship and marketing activities.**

2 Compile an agreed list of your club's sponsorship opportunities.

3 Create and maintain a list of potential sponsor companies.

4 Keep a record of your club's local press coverage.

5 Tailor the advantages of sponsorship for each prospective sponsor, and try to show the benefits this will offer to them.

6 Value each opportunity based on the publicity it generates, its status in the local community and the additional exploitation opportunities it presents.

7 Agree in writing all aspects of the sponsorship.

8 Regard the guaranteed rights as a minimum – try to deliver beyond the sponsor's expectations.

9 Continually try to promote and improve your club's sponsorship opportunities.

10 Plan ahead when sponsorship agreements are coming to the end of their term.

Additional points to remember include:

- Successful sponsorships are mutually beneficial.
- Raising sponsorship is not a one-off activity.
- Always plan ahead.
- Every business or commercial concern is a potential sponsor.
- Keep a record of the media coverage achieved by each property.
- Be flexible.
- Continually try to extend or improve properties.
- Contracts or written agreements help both parties.
- Be positive and understand the benefits that sponsorship can offer.
- Consider not only cash arrangements for sponsorship, but benefits in kind for services that your club would otherwise have to pay for.

Summary

- **Sponsorship is a vital part of the promotion and development of a football club.**

- **Remember that sponsorship is a partnership between the club and the company or individual that is willing to invest.**

- **Clubs must always be able to deliver what they have promised.**

Self testers

1 Give three examples of the types of local companies that might be worth approaching as potential sponsors.

2 How can you exceed a sponsor's expectations?

3 List as many elements as possible that should be included in the basic agreement between a sponsor and the club.

Action plan

How can I start to tackle sponsorship? Attempt to identify and list all of your club's properties and rights that would be of value to potential sponsors.

Chapter 6

LEARNING

Problem solving

THIS CHAPTER WILL:

- Explore the problems and challenges you may face when running your club.
- Look at how to avoid problems.
- Give advice on finding solutions and on who may be able to help.
- Include advice on what to do if the club is losing players, loses its pitch or is hit by bad weather.
- Suggest how to control the behaviour of players, officials and spectators.
- Cover how you can deal with the disbandment of a club and what to do when players fall out.

Administration

Any club or organization needs good administration. Administration provides the framework that allows everything to operate. As we covered throughout the book, in football there are many rules and duties that must be performed to enable the game to run smoothly. Clubs can find themselves in trouble in this area if they are not on top of the administration side of the game. If correspondence is unanswered and registration forms lie around, before you know it the whole administration of the club seems too much to deal with.

Here are some simple rules to help with administration:

1 List what needs doing.
2 Agree who is responsible for what.
3 Keep a record.
4 Reply to correspondence straight away, don't leave it until the deadline.
5 Set time aside to carry out administration duties.
6 Attend training courses in football administration.
7 Don't be afraid to ask for help! If you need advice, phone your league – they would much rather help a club than fine one and, ultimately, lose the club from the league.

If things are not looking good, be up front and tell people:

• Inform other club officials/members – they might be able to help.

• Contact your County FA or relevant association, league and competitors – they may also be of help.

Best Practice Remember that there is always someone who can help so you should never let things get out of hand.

Quote | 'Without the volunteer workforce administering, coaching, and supporting grassroots football, the game would not be able to continue!'

Statistic

Did you know that the conservative estimated value of the volunteer workforce in grassroots football in England is **£500 million** a season?

Financial matters

I once received a phone call from a club secretary, which was along these lines:

Caller: Les, can you help? I need to find a treasurer.

Les: Well, I will see what we can do through our Volunteer Programme.

Caller: No, we are looking for our treasurer who has run off with the club funds!

Financial problems fall into two categories, those similar to the above example and, more predominantly, those when the funds run out. In Chapter 4 we looked at some best practice ideas which should help ensure that you don't run into problems. Possibly the most important point to reiterate is that you need to set a budget so that everyone is aware and there are no surprises. Again, if there are problems tell the people in your club and ask for help.

Quote | 'In England, The FA's commitment to grassroots football is stronger than ever and we are committed to distributing 50 per cent of all profits back into grassroots and non-professional football.'

If your team needs more money, can you list five ways to generate more revenue?

Statistic

In 2003, The FA invested over **£30 million** into amateur/grassroots football.

Lack of players

The most common reason why teams fold during the season is because of a lack of players. Before the season starts, ensure that you have a squad. You will need to sign on at least 14 players because there will always be someone either injured, unavailable through holidays or who has work commitments. Ideally you should have a squad of 15–16 players, but you need to keep them all happy and make certain that everyone gets regular time on the pitch.

Some teams may start with 16 players, but if the same 11 are always picked, when it comes to February the team could go down to 12. In theory, this may work. However, when two players are injured and one is suspended you can soon find yourself struggling.

Be realistic – the reality is that players who may be keen during the nice weather of pre-season may not be so enthusiastic in the cold of mid-winter.

* Look to sign 14–16 players.
* Try to keep everyone happy.
* Be aware of holiday/work periods – if you know them in advance, ask the league for no games on these dates.
* If you are short of players, how can you recruit during the season?
    * Ask existing players to bring a friend.
    * Ask other clubs if they can help you out on a short-term basis.

■ It is important to be able to get hold of extra players quickly. Do you have all the contact details of all your players readily available in case the worst happens and you suddenly have to find extra players at the last minute? If not, make this a priority to do as soon as possible.

Best Practice To make sure that last season's players re-sign, a number of clubs invest in either e-mail or newsletters – in this way everyone connected with the club keeps in contact over the close season and is ready and raring to go once pre-season training arrives.

The club has lost the pitch

You have followed the guidance in Chapters 1 and 3 on planning for the season and your pitch is booked for the season. Yet halfway through the season, your pitch is unavailable. Don't panic!

- Go back to where you originally booked and ask if they have an alternative.

- Ask the league/local County FA or relevant association to help, and ask if they have any contacts.

- Find out if any other club that has its own ground can help you out.

▓   Draw up a list of alternative pitches so that you are prepared if you can't play on your usual home pitch.

Bad weather

The pitch is waterlogged, we can't play!

This will probably happen at least once a season, and it is not a problem. However, when there is a bad winter and fixtures are lost week after week, it can cause a backlog at the end of the season. You will need to consider the following:

- Is the squad big enough because not everyone will be able to play mid-week games?

- Is there an alternative pitch where games can be played?

- Can you identify an evening which would be best for mid-week games and ask the league to programme your games on that evening?
- Can you play any mid-week games at the start of the season when it is still light and enthusiasm is at its highest?

Fallings out

It is a fact that people fall out with each other. In any club or organization, at some stage during the season there will be a disagreement. There are many reasons why this may happen, and they are not all football-related. Some problems may be out of your control, and we don't all have to be friends to be a team. There have been famous cases in professional football where colleagues haven't spoken to each other for years. There is a message here for everyone – the professional players have got on with the job and keep their personal differences away from the changing room and the pitch. This may require you or a colleague to remind players of their responsibility to the team.

▨ Fallings out between players can be quite common during the intensity of a match. Do you have a plan of what to do if this happens?

Behaviour of players, officials and spectators

It is the club's responsibility to ensure good levels of behaviour from players, officials and spectators.

Golden rules:

- Develop a Code of Conduct with players, officials and spectators, or adopt a Code of Conduct.
- Make sure everyone is aware of the Code of Conduct and competition rules.
- If there is a problem, deal with it and use your Code of Conduct. Don't wait for The FA or competition – take responsibility yourselves.

Please remember that in addition to the club rules (Code of Conduct and the Laws of the Game), everyone must operate within the laws of the land at all times.

Quote | 'Club officials must act at all times in the best interest of the game as well as their club. Civil and criminal liability can apply on the football field just like anywhere else. If anyone, including spectators, act outside the law of their legal duties they could face prosecution by a civil law firm.'

Best Practice One club in the north west of England will only allow those players to affiliate who have signed and agreed to the club's code of practice for their acceptable behaviour. Anyone who breaks the code, for example by swearing at the referees, has to pay a fine which is collected and distributed to a chosen local charity at the end of the season.

Disbandment

Despite all of your hard work, it is still possible for the club to fold. If this does happen, make sure that the following administration is in place.

Fixtures

If there is a doubt about the future of the club, advise the County FA and any league or competitions to which the club belongs as soon as possible. Every effort should be made to complete the season's fixtures.

Correspondence

Attend to all outstanding correspondence such as disciplinary or pitch hire matters and the return of cups and trophies.

Financial matters

The following rule is taken directly from The FA in England, but it raises interesting questions for all clubs that may have financial difficulties and as a result, disband.

'Before a club disbands it is essential that all debts and fines are cleared so that players are not prohibited from playing for a new club. Failure to attend to this matter correctly may lead to players being responsible for an equal share of any outstanding amount owed. If there are insufficient funds to pay the outstanding accounts, every member should collectively contribute to the amount required. If there is a surplus, the club rules should be consulted and, in the absence of specific instructions, consideration should be given to making a donation to the County Football Association Benevolent Fund (ask your local association if they have a similar scheme). Whatever the circumstances, an entry should be made in the minutes of the relevant meeting to record the decision taken. Finally, a responsible member should retain the minute book and other club records for a two-year period, and his or her contact details should be passed to the County FA in case of subsequent enquiries about the club.'

Volunteers

One of the main reasons for a club's disbanding is that no one volunteers to run the club. Often in football we are our own worst enemy; one person does everything and, when they leave, no one wants to take on all that responsibility. Therefore, the more volunteers there are to share the workload, the more likely it is that a club will be sustainable. It is vital that, where possible, you follow the advice about volunteers given in Chapter 7.

Statistic

More than **99.5 per cent** of football administrators are volunteers.

Best Practice To make sure that all the volunteers feel part of the club, remember to reward them at end of season award ceremonies. In England, The FA donates 'Volunteer Reward' certificates and distributes over 15,000 copies each year.

Summary

- Be prepared for the types of problems that can regularly occur.

- Have contingencies in place just in case the worst happens.

- Deal with any problem straight away – never ignore an issue and hope it will disappear.

Self testers

1   Your club has a fixture backlog, what should you do?

2   Your two best players at the club are refusing to talk to each other and it is affecting their performance on the pitch. What is the best way to deal with this situation?

3   An injury crisis means that your club is struggling for players and is in danger of having to cancel games. Can you think of a solution to this problem?

Action plan

Which problems should I address first?   Write a bullet-point list of ways to solve your five most common problems. Use the hints and tips in this chapter as well as your own experiences.

Chapter 7

Supporting your volunteers

THIS CHAPTER WILL:
- Look at the recruitment of volunteers.
- Assign roles and responsibilities.
- Show how to reward volunteers.

Football survives thanks to the thousands of volunteers who keep the clubs and leagues thriving.

Quote | 'Being involved in the game doesn't necessarily mean playing, it can just as easily mean cutting the oranges at half-time, ringing in the results at the end of a game, or preparing the pitch.'

Recruitment

Here are six smart moves to help you with your recruitment goals for volunteers.

1 What jobs need to be done?

- Start early and give yourself as much time as possible to recruit your volunteers.

- Make a list of the roles that need filling.

- Are some of the jobs too big for one person?

- Think about sharing out the jobs that demand a lot of time.

2 Define the tasks

- What is involved in each job?

- Write a brief role description.

- Make sure you are honest. Let people know what you want them to do, and what they are taking on.

- Speak to the people who carried out each job last season.

- Look at the 'Roles and responsibilities' section on p. 98 for some ideas about how to describe jobs.

- Leave time for some pre-season training!

3 Who could do the jobs?

- Compare the skills required with the potential volunteers.

- Does every volunteer really have to know about football?

- Decide which is the most important factor – skills or experience?

- How can you help people to gain the skills they need?

4 The search is on!

- Where will you find somebody who has the skills for each role?

- Use the network – parents, friends within the club, or contacts outside the club.

- Target your search to find the right person for the right job.

- Gather information about the skills within the club or among your supporters.

5 Let people know that they are needed

- Sell the benefits of being part of your club.
- Let people know what help you need.
- Remember that people like to be asked – don't be shy!
- Match jobs to the time that people have to give. Volunteers are much more likely to stick at it if they are not overloaded.

6 Start as you mean to go on

- Make it easy to join.
- Ease people into their new jobs with plenty of support from their teammates.
- Well-supported new recruits will soon want to play their full part in the team.
- Look at the 'Getting off to a good start' checklist on p. 106.

Roles and responsibilities

Quote | 'I was given a clear list of my roles and responsibilities; this made it much easier for me to see how my job fitted in with everybody else on the committee.'

▓   Write down the names of the roles from pages 99–106 and use them to describe the jobs within your club.

Having identified the key roles in your club, use this information to:

- Check that there is not too much duplication between jobs, or that a really important task has not slipped through the net.

- Explain to potential volunteers what is involved in each job.

- Match potential volunteers to jobs they will enjoy.

- See how each job links to another – people like to see how their work fits into the bigger picture.

- Review the roles within the club or league. Is this the most effective way to get the work done, or are some roles there because they always have been?

- Explore the possibility of breaking down time-consuming jobs into smaller parts.

Statistic

There are around **half a million** volunteers involved in grassroots football in England alone.

Here are some examples of roles and responsibilities for typical club positions. They may not match the jobs that exist in your club but they will provide you with a framework and ideas.

Club chairperson

Who will I be responsible to?
The main committee.

Who will I be responsible for?
Nobody.

What is the remit of the club chairperson?
To chair the committee meetings and AGM. Assist the secretary to produce the agendas. Head the committee in making decisions for the benefit of the whole club, including disciplinary matters.

What else can you tell me about the job?
As the chair of the club, it is essential that you are a strong leader and that you can be objective. As the supporting officer to the secretary, it is useful for you to have access to a telephone. You may wish to attend a specific training course on how to chair/run meetings.

How much time will I need to give to the job?
Two to three hours per month for meetings.

What sorts of tasks are involved?
- Chairing committee meetings/AGM.
- Agreeing monthly agenda for committee meetings and the AGM.

Club secretary

Who will I be responsible to?
The main committee, through the chairperson.

Who will I be responsible for?
The assistant secretary.

What is the remit of the club secretary?

The main purpose of this job is that of principal administrator for the club. The club secretary carries out or delegates all of the administrative duties that enable the club and its members to function effectively. The club secretary is a pivotal role within the club, with a close involvement in the general running of the club. The secretary and his/her assistant provide the main point of contact for people within and outside the club on most aspects of the club's activities.

What else can you tell me about the job?

As the first point of contact with the club, it is helpful if the secretary can be available to take phone calls during the working day. This is a demanding, high profile job that has a major impact on the efficient and effective management of the club. The secretary has contact with a wide range of people from within and outside the club. Representation of the club at outside meetings provides the opportunity to find out what is going on at league and county level, and this could be a platform for future volunteering opportunities.

How much time will I need to give to the job?

Approximately eight hours each week, and many of these will be at the weekend and in the evenings, although this will depend on the size of the club.

What sorts of tasks are involved?

- Attending league meetings.
- Affiliating the club to the County FA.
- Affiliating the club to the league(s).
- Registering players to the league(s).
- Dealing with correspondence.
- Organizing and booking match facilities for the season.
- Organizing the club AGM and other club meetings.

- Representing the club at outside meetings at the direction of the main committee.

Team manager

Who will I be responsible to?
Club committee.

Who will I be responsible for?
A particular team, for example, the Under 13 team.

What is the remit of the team manager?
The main purpose of the job is to ensure that the club provides a team to compete in the district youth league and cup competitions. The manager is responsible for all aspects of activity regarding the age group. The manager is permitted to engage assistants provided that they meet the membership requirements of the club.

What else can you tell me about the job?
The club will usually require some formal football coaching qualification. For example, in England, a team manager should hold the minimum FA qualification of The FA Club Coach (including first aid award). The club

will often assist and support you in obtaining this award during the season if you do not already have the qualification. Depending on the resources of the club, you may receive an allowance for telephone calls. Other club officials and team managers are always available for any assistance or advice. Ensure that you are issued a club first aid kit and, if at all possible, have completed basic first aid training. The club will provide all playing kit and match and training equipment.

How much time will I need to give to the job?

Team activities on match day will depend on the venue for the game and take approximately four hours. Coaching and training sessions at the club each week take around two hours. Other duties are spread across the week such as telephone calls and other administration tasks and will take around four hours.

What sorts of tasks are involved?

Weekly

- Team selection.
- Organization of coaching and training at the club once a week.
- Organization of transport for team matches.
- Team kit and equipment (including laundry – parents usually take turns).
- Reporting results to the club secretary after matches.

Monthly

- Team accounts.
- Monthly club team managers' meeting.

Once each season

- End of season report to club committee.

Fund-raising secretary

Who will I be responsible to?

The main committee.

Who will I be responsible for?

Fund-raising committee or main committee.

What is the remit of the fund-raising secretary?

To work with the media secretary (if there is one – see below) to raise awareness of the club in the local area, with the aim of increasing the amount of sponsorship (and therefore funding) that the club receives.

What else can you tell me about the job?

As the fund-raising secretary, it is essential to have good organizational skills, be innovative, enthusiastic and prepared to make a regular time commitment. It would be useful if you have experience of completing grant applications. Training courses are often available on a variety of subjects and will be managed through County FAs or relevant local associations.

How much time will I need to give to the job?

On average, three to four hours each week, but this could rise to eight hours around the time of fund-raising events.

What sorts of tasks are involved?

- Applying for grants/sponsorships or other forms of financial assistance from organizations such as Sport England/Football Foundation, Local Authorities (in England) or commercial companies.
- Co-ordinating two major fund-raising events each year, for example, race night and presentation evening.
- Ensuring events and activities are properly licensed with local authorities and/or customs and excise.
- Promoting fund-raising activities through the press (where there is no PR officer).

- Making sure that funds are properly accounted for and information is passed on to the treasurer.
- Sale of lottery style draw or raffle tickets on a regular basis, probably weekly.

Media secretary

Who will I be responsible to?
The main committee.

Who will I be responsible for?
PR/Media committee (if the club has one).

What is the remit of the media secretary?
To raise the profile of the club in the local community and to be available to talk to local media. To co-ordinate weekly match reports for all teams and age groups for forwarding to the local press, and to edit the match day programme (in larger clubs).

What else can you tell me about the job?
As the media officer, it is essential to have good communication skills and an ability to produce coherent match reports, press releases, etc. Access to a fax, telephone and computer are necessary. Training courses are often available on a variety of subjects and will be managed through County FAs or relevant local associations.

How much time will I need to give to the job?
Approximately two to four hours per week.

What sorts of tasks are involved?
- Producing weekly match reports for inclusion in the local paper.
- Producing a club news sheet twice a season.
- Co-ordinating production of the programme for home games.
- Writing general interest stories about the club for local press.

- Making sure that the club is featured in locally-produced sports magazines.

Treasurer

Who will I be responsible to?

The main committee.

Who will I be responsible for?

Match/Training fees collector.

What is the remit of the treasurer?

The main purpose of this job is to look after the finances of the club and regularly report back to members.

What else can you tell me about the job?

The treasurer must be well organized, able to keep records, careful when handling money and cheques, scrupulously honest, able to answer questions in meetings, confident at handling figures and prepared to take instant decisions when necessary. Training courses are often available on a variety of subjects and will be managed through County FAs or relevant local associations.

How much time will I need to give to the job?

Approximately two to three hours per week.

What sorts of tasks are involved?

- Collecting subscriptions and all money due to the organization.
- Paying the bills and recording information.
- Keeping up-to-date records of all financial transactions.
- Ensuring that all cash and cheques are promptly deposited in the bank or building society.
- Making sure that funds are spent properly.
- Issuing receipts for all money received, and recording this information.

- Reporting regularly to the committee about the financial position.

- Preparing a year end statement of accounts to present to the auditors.

- Arranging for the statement of accounts to be audited.

- Presenting an end of year financial report to the AGM.

- Financial planning, including producing an annual budget and monitoring it throughout the year.

- Helping to prepare and submit any statutory documents that are required.

Even if these duties are delegated to a professional officer (i.e. paid accountant), the treasurer is still ultimately responsible. It is up to the treasurer to make sure that any delegated work is carried out properly.

Statistic

Research suggests that there are more than **200,000** people assisting in the administrative duties of football clubs in England.

Getting off to a good start

Quote | 'I've learnt so much since I got involved with the mini-soccer programme.'

Checklist

- Make sure that each new volunteer has a 'buddy', somebody they can ask if they are in doubt about anything to do with their new job – ideally, somebody who has done that job before.

- Check that volunteers have received a list of their roles and responsibilities, and that they understand exactly what they are supposed to do.

- Introduce volunteers to the people with whom they will be working.

- Provide a list of names, addresses and telephone numbers of volunteers' key contacts within and outside the club.

- Provide details of meetings or events that volunteers will need to attend in the first few months of their job.

- Provide details of key dates, for example, the closing date for league affiliations.

- Ensure that volunteers know where to find the things they need to do the job (and how to work them), for instance, line-marking equipment, first aid kit, computer, paperwork, stationery.

- Do volunteers have all the skills needed to do the job? Could somebody within the club help by 'showing them the ropes'? Or maybe volunteers could attend an administration course and learn from people from other clubs?

- Provide written details of expenses that may be claimed and how to claim them.

- If appropriate to the job, provide information on club financial procedures, confidentiality, and other operating policies such as child protection practices.

- Tell volunteers how they are getting on – provide some feedback on progress. People like to know how they are performing and to learn positively from any mistakes they might have made.

- Committee chairpersons should take time to get to know new committee members, briefing them about committee procedures, terms of reference, and responsibilities.

Recognition and reward

Quote | 'It would be nice if, just once in a while, somebody said thank you.'

During the season

Recognizing and rewarding the hard work and enthusiasm of not only the players, but also the team of volunteers and helpers is something that should go on throughout the season.

- Take the trouble to say 'thank you'.
- Attempt to raise the profile of volunteers and helpers throughout the club, for example, having a 'helper of the month' award.

Best Practice If you can, have some specially designed thank-you cards made for your club. These will cost little, but will be much appreciated by the volunteers who receive them.

End of season

On or off the field, as the end of the season approaches you can look back over the year and celebrate the successes or analyse the things that didn't go quite so well. This is the time to think how it will be even better next year!

At the end of the season, make sure you do something special to recognize the time and effort given to the club by the volunteers such as:

- An awards evening.
- A social event for volunteers and helpers.
- A volunteers' team talk to begin the planning for next season.

Quote | 'I wanted to put something back into the game, I really enjoy being involved.'

Rewarding special achievements

There will be some volunteers and helpers who deserve a special award. This may be for a number of reasons:

- **They never let you or the club down; they are always there even though their role may not be seen as high profile.**
- **They took on a new role and made great efforts to develop the skills to do it well.**
- **They are an example of good practice that the club wishes to promote, for instance, a young person who has taken on a voluntary role.**

Try to think of a prize or gift that is appropriate to the individual, for example, a youngster might not appreciate a meal for two at a local restaurant, but the parent who has staffed the refreshments stand every Saturday throughout the season would welcome being waited on! A youngster might appreciate some sports kit, or tickets for a professional league game.

List five prizes or gifts that might be appropriate for the volunteers at your club. Do some research to see if local companies would be willing to donate any of the items on your list. To illustrate, the restaurant near your club may be willing to give a meal for two prize to show its support for your club and to gain some publicity.

Perhaps your club has a trophy designated for the off-the-field team members which can be awarded annually. Make a special occasion of presenting awards, perhaps an awards evening or at the AGM.

Schools are usually pleased to hear about their pupils' out-of-school achievements. It may be possible to arrange to present your 'Young Volunteer of the Year' with their prize at a school assembly.

Raising the profile of volunteers

Quote | '. . . don't worry if you don't know anything about football, there are all sorts of jobs that need doing . . .'

Use your club newsletter to publicize all of the work that goes on behind the scenes. Feature two or three people in each newsletter, perhaps in an interview style, and ask them about their role, how they became involved, and the things they enjoy when helping out at the club.

Next time the photographer arrives to take a team photograph make certain that the volunteers and helpers' team is included in the picture.

They might even like to wear some club T-shirts or baseball caps to give them a sense of involvement. If the players award a 'Team Helper of the Month' award, make sure a photograph of the winner appears on the notice board.

FA Football Workforce

In England, The FA has recognized the vital role of volunteers in clubs at every level, and have developed a volunteer programme (Football Workforce) which expands upon the issues raised in this chapter. For more information contact The FA, your county FA directly, or visit the website **www.TheFA.com**.

Below are the case studies of four volunteers who have become involved in different areas of a football club.

June Kelly

I started coaching when I was 13. I used to help out at my old primary school and youth club. When injury forced me to stop playing, I decided to start coaching on a regular basis instead, so that I could still be involved in the game.

I coach the school team as well as being a manager and coach of Abraham Moss Warriors Under 12 and Under 13 girls. I also coach at Abraham Moss Warriors soccer centre for children aged 6–14. I attend league meetings and arrange sponsorship, in addition to the recruitment and training of parents and volunteers.

I pride myself on the club's achievement with Charter Club Standard status, as well as encouraging children and parents from different nationalities to become actively involved in football. At the present time, we have members from 14 different countries. The thing I enjoy the most is watching a child improve in confidence when playing football. At Abraham Moss Warriors we are like one large, happy family.

Steve Williams

I started out in football at the age of 13, playing for a school team. Thankfully I joined the youth team soon after, which was started by one of the senior boys at the school. This gave me the interest, apart from watching football on television, to get more involved as I grew older.

Unfortunately, the team disbanded after two years and it was suggested that I considered a role as a referee for youth matches. At the age of 16, I passed the exam with flying colours and was instantly recruited on to several leagues. This is how I began to meet so many club, league and county officials, which would provide a good base from which to move forward in later years.

At the age of 19, I began co-managing an Under 18 youth team, connected with a non-league club. The following season I was asked if I would consider becoming the club's match secretary for the first team. This was quite a step up at this stage, but one I was really keen on, capped by the team's promotion in my first season in the role. This involved travelling with the team to every match, home and away, exchanging teamsheets and providing the link between the team manager and the club committee.

I remained at the club for ten years in all, before a power struggle within the committee meant I was not enjoying the role anymore, and it was time to move on. I did not know what would happen, but because of the experience and knowledge I had previously built up, another club asked me to become their secretary, a position I have remained in for the last 13 years. The club now runs 23 teams and has just been awarded FA Community Club status.

My role involves dealing with all correspondence, initially from The FA, leagues and County FA, providing a vision for the youth managers to aspire to because they are potentially the next committee members, registering and affiliating all teams into respective leagues and competitions, and providing general advice and guidance throughout the club.

In addition to this, I've been managing a youth team for the past ten years on Sundays, which provides a real alternative to other club duties and gives me a perspective of how parents and players feel within the club. I still register each season as a referee for the occasional match when time permits.

Football has given me a real sense of both ownership and friendship, and taught me about responsibilities from a relatively young age into adulthood and parenthood.

Kath Tranter

As a player in the early days of the Women's FA there were no teams where I lived. Fortunately, I have a football-mad father who gave up his Sundays to drive me to and from matches. The Women's FA then introduced a rule that said you can only play for a club within an 80-km (50-mile) radius of your home, which again left me with no club. The only choice was to start a club of my own. Having found the players and managers, I could not get anyone to carry out the administration roles, so I ended up doing them myself. That was how I started.

Getting into the job made me realize how incorrectly some things were done (not having any age structure, treating cuts on the playing field by using the same sponge and water that someone else had cleaned their boots with), yet I appreciated how much work other people had done, with little or no support, to get leagues and competitions started. As the game grew, many things altered and progressed and I was able, through The FA, to educate myself towards better practices. I can now, within my own club, promote these practices to the players and other volunteers through the coach education system – regularly sending them to emergency aid, child protection and coaching courses.

I don't believe that you can measure what we get out of it. For me it is the friends that I made, the things that I have learnt, and the fact that I can see how many players, leagues and competitions there are now compared to when I first started. In a nutshell, I continued to do it, hopefully giving something back as someone did for me many years ago.

Rashid Abba

I came to England in 1976 from Malawi, central Africa, and settled in Leicester. I played football in the street most of the time with my friends, with no coaching, no proper equipment, no facilities and no structured football in either school or leagues.

I have never played youth football in organized leagues in either Malawi or England. I first started playing adult football at the age of 19 for an Asian club called Red Star, before moving to other ethnic clubs in the area. I was the first Asian player to play in the Leicestershire Senior League.

In 1990, when I was on work placement at Leicester City Football Club, I became involved in coaching in schools and during holiday courses. I gained valuable experience working at a professional club and really enjoyed my time working with children from different backgrounds, and also for voluntary organizations. As the work placement was only for a year and there was no full-time vacancy, I had to leave the club but I continued coaching in both a voluntary and paid capacity while at the same time working as a youth leader for a Local Authority organization. I have since rejoined Leicester City Football in the Community, but remain a volunteer supporting local grassroots clubs.

Much of my work has been in deprived, multicultural, inner-city areas. My role is to act as a link between the club and the diverse groups that make up the community it serves. I have enjoyed meeting and working with a wide variety of people and look forward to the challenge of continuing and developing the success I have experienced so far.

Summary

- Think about who you need to recruit and the best place to recruit from.

- Carry out a skill audit.

- Draw up and agree the roles for each position.

- Ensure new volunteers receive support.

- Remember to say 'thank you'.

- Develop a recognition programme.

- Use every opportunity to raise the profile of volunteers.

Self testers

1 Name three ways in which you can reward your volunteers.

2 Attempt to identify as many tasks of the club secretary role as you can.

3 Which individuals involved in your club make up the network of possible volunteers?

Action plan

How do I go about recruiting volunteers? Put together a plan that outlines the number of volunteers you will need, the roles of these people, and a description of their responsibilities.

Chapter 8

Development and progress for the future

THIS CHAPTER WILL:
- Help you to think about the future of your club.
- Look at how to produce a club development plan.

Why produce a development plan?

A club development plan will help the club to move forward and is a vital document to provide the club with focus, and to assist in raising funds. A simple plan can also open up potential grant aid opportunities which will ensure that you have the finances to put the plan into action.

Quote | 'A development plan is an essential part of ensuring that your club progresses and makes the most of its potential. Make this a priority as it can trigger opportunities such as funding and identifying more sponsors.'

Planning ahead is the easiest way to help any club to develop. The plan will provide a development framework that will require the co-operation of all of those within the club. When producing a club development plan, your club will need to identify:

- **The aims of the club within the plan.**
- **The objectives of the club within the plan.**
- **The methods that will be used.**
- **Who will be responsible.**
- **The timescales in which objectives can be achieved.**
- **The financial resources required.**

Before your club writes this plan you will need to identify:

- **Where you are now.**
- **Where you want to be.**
- **How you will get there.**

Best Practice When producing the plan, involve at least two or three people to ensure that it meets the needs of the whole club.

Now that you have some ideas about what you would like to achieve, you have to decide how this will happen. Here are two examples of how to structure a club development plan.

Statistic
Over **250,000** children in England play mini-soccer.

Aim
To stage an annual mini-soccer festival.

Objective
To run an annual mini-soccer festival that includes girls and boys aged 7–11 from local schools.

Method
In partnership with the local authority or relevant organization, contact schools and organize the festival.

Responsibilities
John – contact local authority regarding pitches and facilities.

Paul – organize coaches and referees.

Donna – organize publicity (flyers), marketing, and produce certificates.

Timescale
Within six months – to be held in the summer.

Facilities and resources
- **Venue large enough to hold six mini-soccer pitches.**
- **Small-sided goals.**
- **Match balls.**
- **Officials.**

Costings
Venue: _____

Goals: _____

Officials: _____

Balls: Borrow from local authority.

Prizes: _____

Certificates: _____

Revenue
Fee per team: _____

Aim
To develop youth football within the club.

Objective
To set up a mini-soccer team (mixed).

Method
To invite girls and boys to regular mini-soccer sessions at the club.

Responsibilities
Julie – produce club leaflet and invitation letter.
Tom – purchase resources (see below).
Danny – team coach responsible for selection and training.

Timescale
By May 2005.

Facilities and resources
• Balls.
• First aid kit (if club does not already have one).
• Training equipment for example cones and bibs (suitable for younger players).

Costings
Balls: _____

Training equipment: _____

Administration
    (leaflets/letters/postage): _____

Revenue
Fee per player: _____

Some areas that the club may wish to consider when writing a club development plan include:

- Recruitment/retention of players and volunteers.
- Developing a mini-soccer section.
- Links with local schools.
- Links with local girls/boys clubs.
- Developing new teams, for example, Under 8s, Veterans.
- Exit routes:
    - How do we move teenagers up to the adult game?
    - What happens if an academy approaches a player?
- Volunteer support and development.

- Coach education.
- Disability programme.
- Links to other local clubs.
- Communication plan.

As a club, you will decide your priorities by producing a plan, and it will help you to achieve your goals. Remember every club should have a plan!

▓ Within your club, who may be the best help in putting together a plan? Try to get people who approach the game from different perspectives, i.e. a parent, a member of the committee and an experienced player.

Benefits of planning

- Provides focus for the club.
- Everyone can see the plan and take ownership.
- It can help obtain funding.
- Achieving your FA Charter Standard (England only).

Quote | 'The best plans are often the simplest.'

Keep your plan SMART:

Specific
Measurable
Achievable
Realistic
Time measured.

Summary

- **Every club should have a club development plan.**

- **More than one person should be involved in writing the plan.**

- **Think about the areas of the club that need to be involved.**

- **Before you write the plan, identify:**

  - **Where you are now.**

  - **Where you want to be.**

  - **How you will get there.**

Self testers

1 Outline the basic structure for the sections of the plan.
2 Think of all the areas that should be included.
3 What does SMART stand for?

Action plan

How do I start my development plan? Consider your club and the areas that require focus for development. Use the structure provided in this chapter to start writing your plan. Remember to involve other people.

Chapter 9

LEARNING

Health and safety

THIS CHAPTER WILL:
- Outline basic issues surrounding health and safety.
- Provide a useful guide to risk assessment.
- Highlight the importance of goalpost safety.

Quote | 'Safety of players, officials and spectators is the number one priority.'

The safety of everyone involved in football must be a priority. While there will always be accidents, particularly in a contact sport like football, it is our duty to do all we can to make the sport safe. Let's look at what can be done.

First aid

The club must make sure that:

- Every team has a qualified first aider present.
- There is always an appropriately stocked and suitable first aid kit. Remember to check it regularly and always replace any items used.

- There is a phone available at all games and training. At most games now everyone has a mobile phone (and that's just the Under 8 team!), but make sure that there is a signal and, if not, find out where the nearest landline phone is situated.

- Make sure you can give directions to where you are, in case you need to call an ambulance – 'down the lane, over the bushes and through the hole in the fence' won't be much good!

Statistic

The FA trains over **40,000** people a year in first aid and the treatment of injuries.

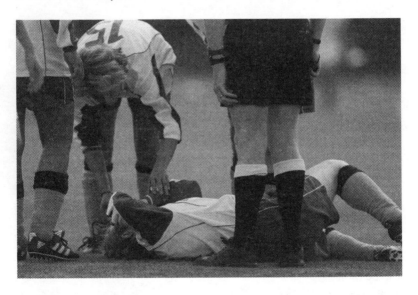

Risk assessment

At the start of each season, you should carry out a risk assessment on the venue used by the club. This should be regularly checked and updated, especially if circumstances change. It is also advisable to do a similar check on new situations, for example a trip away to a tournament or festival.

Risk assessment form

Venue: _____

Date of check: _____

Name and position of person doing check: _____

Player/Training area
Check that the area and surroundings are free from obstacles.

Is the area fit and appropriate for activity?   Yes ☐ No ☐

(Please outline the hazard, who may be at risk, and action taken, if any.)

Goalposts
Are the goalposts safe and appropriate for activity? (Please refer to 'Goalpost safety guidelines' on p. 128)   Yes ☐ No ☐

(Please detail unsafe equipment, who may be at risk, and action taken, if any.)

Players
Check that the players' register is up to date with medical information and contact details.

Is/are the register(s) in order?   Yes ☐ No ☐

(Please outline current state, and action taken, if any).

Check that players are appropriately attired for the activity.

Are players appropriately attired and safe for activity?   Yes ☐ No ☐

(Please detail unsafe equipment/attire, and action taken, if any.)

Emergency points
Check that emergency vehicles can access facilities, a working telephone is available with access to emergency numbers, and that exit points are clear.

Are emergency points checked and operational?   Yes ☐ No ☐
(Please outline the issues and action taken, if any.)

Is a working telephone available? Yes ☐ No ☐
(Please outline the issues, and action taken, if any.)

Safety information
Check that evacuation procedures are published and posted up
for all to see. Ensure that volunteers and staff have access to
information relating to health and safety.

Are emergency procedures published and accessible to those with
responsibility for sessions in the club? Yes ☐ No ☐
(Please detail any information that is missing, and action taken, if
any.)

Does the club need to take any further action?
(If yes, please specify) Yes ☐ No ☐

Signed: _____ Date: _____

Name (print): _____

Goalposts

It is of the greatest importance that you check the goalposts, before
every game, at half-time and during training. There have been a number
of child deaths caused by goalposts toppling over, so please, please
follow the goalpost safety guidelines below. In England, The FA has
produced literature on this issue, and to find out more you can contact
your local County FA or visit **www.TheFA.com**.

Goalpost safety guidelines

The FA, along with the Department for Culture, Media and Sport, the
Health and Safety Executive and the British Standards Institution (BSI),
would like to draw your attention to the following guidelines for the safe
use of goalposts.

Too many serious injuries and fatalities have occurred in recent years as a result of unsafe or incorrect use of goalposts. Safety is always of paramount importance and everyone in football must play their part to prevent similar incidents occurring in the future.

- For safety reasons, goalposts of any size (including those which are portable and not installed permanently at a pitch or practice field) must always be anchored securely to the ground.

  - Portable goalposts must be secured by the use of chain anchors or appropriate anchor weights to prevent them from toppling forward.

  - It is essential that under no circumstances should children or adults be allowed to climb, swing or play on the structures of the goalposts.

  - Particular attention is drawn to the fact that, if not properly assembled and secured, portable goalposts may topple over.

  - Regular inspections of goalposts should be carried out to check that they are properly maintained.

- Portable goalposts should not be left in place after use. They should be dismantled and removed to a place of secure storage.

- It is strongly recommended that nets should only be secured by plastic hooks or tape and not by metal cup hooks. Any metal cup hooks should, if possible, be removed and replaced. New goalposts should not be purchased if they include metal cup hooks that cannot be replaced.

- Goalposts that are homemade or have been altered from their original size or construction should not be used. These have been the cause of a number of deaths and injuries.

- Guidelines to prevent toppling:

  - Follow manufacturer's guidelines in assembling goalposts.

  - Before use, adults should:

    - Ensure each goal is anchored securely in its place.

    - Exert a significant downward force on the crossbar.

    - Exert a significant backward force on both upright posts.

    - Exert a significant forward force on both upright posts.

Plan and prepare thoroughly when travelling to away matches and always have a contact number for the opposing team.

If it's vital the team gets a new kit, you'll need to plan your finances properly and make the most of sponsorship opportunities.

Lots of companies want to get involved in football sponsorship, be specific about who you are targeting when looking to raise money for the club.

Manage your volunteers well, make sure that where possible they are doing the job best suited to them and that they feel valued and are rewarded.

To improve every aspect of the club, including facilities, you will need to have a development plan in place.

You should have a qualified First Aider with your team at all times.

These actions must be repeated until it is established that the structure is secure. If not, alternative goals/pitches must be used.

> For reference, you should note that The FA and BSI have developed a standard for future purchases (PAS 36:2000) available from BSI. It is hoped that this will be developed into a full British Standard in due course.

Remember to use all equipment, not just goalposts, safely at all times.

■ Check the goalposts at your own club very carefully. Do they conform to all the safety points mentioned above? If not, stop using them immediately. Designate someone to regularly check the goalposts, not just on match days, but at regular intervals between matches.

Training venue

When carrying out your risk assessment here are some things to look out for:

- Are there any obstacles, for example, wall bars in a gym or radiators?
- For children, is there a well-lit entrance?
- Is the lighting covered or, if a ball hits the lights, will they break?
- Check the changing rooms; make sure they're not slippery.

Best Practice Remember to keep checking – I once played in a gym that had condensation on the floor when it was cold outside and made the area like a skating rink!

Home venue

At home, check:

- The pitch, particularly during extreme weather conditions. (Also check for rubbish and other potential dangers.)
- Goalposts – remember goalpost safety.
- If using corner flags, that they confer with the laws of the game. They should be over 1.5m (5ft) out of the ground with no sharp edges.
- The changing rooms, including the shower area.

Quote | 'A little tip: carry flip-flops in your kit bag to wear in the changing room and shower – as well as preventing the spread of infections, it is much nicer!'

Equipment

- Check the footballs; ensure that there are no splits in the leather that could cause a cut.

Players

- Check if anyone has any injuries or is feeling unwell.
- Make sure that jewellery is removed, and that shin guards are worn – this includes when training.
- Do a warm up and a cool down to help prevent injuries.

Dealing with accidents

Unfortunately, accidents will happen and, if they do, remember to:

1 Stay calm but act swiftly and observe the situation. Is there any danger of further injuries?

2 Listen to what the injured person is saying.

3 Alert the first aider who should take appropriate action for minor injuries.

4 Call the emergency services in the event of an injury needing specialist treatment.

5 Deal with the rest of the group, and ensure that they are adequately supervised.

6 Make sure you do not move someone with major injuries. Wait for the emergency medics.

7 Contact the injured person's parent/guardian.

8 Complete an accident report form.

Incident/Accident report form

Name of club _____

1 Site where the accident took place _____

2 Name of person in charge of session/competition _____

3 Name of injured person _____

4 Address of injured person _____

5 Date and time of incident/accident _____

6 Nature of incident/accident _____

7 Give details of how and precisely where the accident took place. Describe what activity was taking place (e.g. training programme, getting changed) _____

_____

_____

8 Give full details of the action taken including any first aid treatment and the name(s) of the first aider(s) _____

_____

_____

9 Were any of the following contacted?

Police   Yes ☐ No ☐
Ambulance   Yes ☐ No ☐
Parent/Guardian Yes ☐ No ☐

10 What happened to the injured person following the accident (e.g. went home, went to hospital, carried on with session)?

11 All of the above facts are a true and accurate record of the incident/accident.

Signed: _____   Date: _____

Name (print): _____

Summary

- Ensure you have qualified first aiders.

- First aid kits should be checked and appropriately stocked.

- Always have a phone to hand, and know directions to where you are.

- Carry out risk assessments.

- Always ensure goalpost safety.

- Check your training and match venues.

- Check your equipment.

- Make sure players are free from injuries.

- Ensure players are appropriately dressed.

- Remember to include a warm up.

- If an accident does happen, follow the procedures, and keep a record.

Self testers

1 What are the four key elements regarding club first aid?

2 How often does the club need to review its risk assessment of the home venue?

3 What are the four key safety checks that must be performed by an adult to prevent goalposts from toppling over?

Action plan

I want to see how safe our club venue is Using the
template on p. 127, complete a risk assessment of your club's
home venue.

Conclusion

Football is a great game, and I can honestly say that being involved in running clubs has given me thousands of hours of fun and a real sense of achievement.

This book has hopefully provided you with plenty of advice and practical ideas that will assist you and your club. So to recap:

- There are many reasons to start a club, all of them worthwhile – so do it!
- Like lots of things, the first step is often the hardest but there are many people and organizations only too willing to help and provide support.
- Contact your County FA or relevant organization for help and advice.
- Keep on top of your club administration.
- Set a budget, and stick to it. Remember to keep financial records.
- Look for a sponsor, and develop partnerships with local companies.
- If you have a problem, don't be afraid to ask for help.

- Volunteers are vital, so look after them.
- Keep health and safety paramount in your thoughts.
- Get a club development plan in place – this provides focus and ownership.

I hope you have found some of the advice and tips in this book useful. Most importantly, I hope that you will now put the ideas to good use by getting involved in this great game. All best wishes for the future, and remember to keep enjoying it.

Appendix 1: Example suggestions for Club Rules

1 Name

The club shall be called _____ Football Club (the club).

2 Objects

The object of the club shall be to arrange Association Football matches and social activities for its members.

3 Status of rules

These rules (the Club Rules) form a binding agreement between each member of the club.

Rules and regulations

a   The club shall have the status of an Affiliated Member Club of The Football Association by virtue of its affiliation to/membership of The Football Association. The rules and regulations of the Football Association Limited and parent County Football Association and any league or competition to which the club is affiliated for the time being shall be deemed to be incorporated into the Club Rules.

b   No alteration to the Club Rules shall be effective without prior written approval by the parent association.

c   The club will also abide by The Football Association's Child Protection Policies and Procedures, Codes of Conduct and the Equal Opportunities and Anti-Discrimination Policy.

Club membership

a   The members of the club from time to time shall be those persons listed in the register of members (the Membership Register), which shall be maintained by the club secretary.

b   Any person who wishes to be a member must apply on the Membership Application Form and deliver it to the club. Election to membership shall be at the sole discretion of the club committee. Membership shall become effective upon an applicant's name being entered in the Membership Register.

c   In the event of a member's resignation or expulsion, his or her name shall be removed from the Membership Register.

d   The Football Association and County Association shall be given access to the Membership Register on demand.

Annual membership fee

a   An annual fee payable by each member shall be determined from time to time by the club committee. Any fee shall be payable on a successful application for membership and annually by each member. Fees shall not be repayable.

b   The club committee shall have the authority to levy further subscriptions from the members as are reasonably necessary to fulfil the objects of the club.

Resignation and expulsion

a   A member shall cease to be a member of the club if, and from the date on which, he/she gives notice to the club committee of their resignation. A member whose annual membership fee or further subscription is more than two months in arrears shall be deemed to have resigned.

b   The club committee shall have the power to expel a member when, in their opinion, it would not be in the interests of the club for them to remain a member. There shall be no appeal procedures.

c A member who resigns or is expelled shall not be entitled to claim any, or a share of any, of the club property.

Club Committee

a The club committee shall consist of the following club officers: chairperson, vice-chairperson, treasurer, secretary and minutes secretary. Plus, up to five other members, elected at an Annual General Meeting.

b Each club officer and club committee member shall hold office from the date of appointment until the next Annual General Meeting unless otherwise resolved at a Special General Meeting. One person may hold no more than two positions of club officer at any time. The club committee shall be responsible for the management of all the affairs of the club. Decisions of the club committee shall be made by a simple majority of those attending the club committee meeting. The chairperson of the club committee meeting shall have a casting vote in the event of a tie. Meetings of the club committee shall be chaired by the _____ or in their absence the _____. The quorum for the transaction of business of the club committee shall be for three.

c Decisions of the club committee at meetings shall be entered into the minute book of the club to be maintained by the club secretary.

d Any member of the club committee may call a meeting of the club committee by giving not less than seven days' notice to all members of the club committee. The club committee shall hold not less than four meetings a year.

e An outgoing member of the club committee may be re-elected. Any vacancy on the club committee which arises between Annual General Meetings shall be filled by a member proposed by one and seconded by another of the remaining club committee members and approved by a simple majority of the remaining club committee members.

f   Save as provided for in the rules and regulations of The Football Association to which the club is affiliated, the club committee shall have the power to decide all questions and disputes arising in respect of any issue concerning the club rules.

Annual and Special General Meetings

a   An Annual General Meeting (AGM) shall be held each year to:

     i   Receive a report of the activities of the club over the previous year.

     ii   Receive a report of the club's finances over the previous year.

     iii   Elect the members of the club committee.

     iv   Consider any other business.

b   Nominations for the election of members as club officers or as members of the club committee shall be made in writing by the proposer and seconder, both of whom must be existing members of the club, to the club secretary not less than 21 days before the AGM. Notice of any resolution to be proposed at the AGM shall be given in writing to the club secretary not less than 21 days before the meeting.

c   A Special General Meeting (SGM) may be called at any time by the Committee and shall be called within 21 days of the receipt by the club secretary of a requisition in writing signed by not less than five members stating the purposes for which the meeting is required and the resolutions proposed. Business at an SGM may be any business that may be transacted at an AGM.

d   The secretary shall send to each member at their last known address written notice of the date of a General Meeting together with the resolutions to be proposed at least 14 days before the Meeting.

e   The quorum for a General Meeting shall be _____.

f   The _____, or in their absence a member selected by the club committee, shall take the chair. Each member present shall have one vote and resolutions shall be passed by a simple majority. In the event of an equality of votes the chairperson of the Meeting shall have a casting vote.

g   The club secretary, or in their absence a member of the club committee, shall enter Minutes of General Meetings into the minute book of the club.

Club teams

At its first meeting following each AGM, the club committee shall appoint a club member to be responsible for each of the club's football teams. The appointed members shall be responsible for managing the affairs of the team. The appointed members shall present a written report of the activities of the team to the club committee at its last meeting prior to an AGM.

Club finances

a   A bank account shall be opened and maintained in the name of the club (the Club Account). Designated account signatories shall be the club chairperson, the club secretary and the treasurer. No sum shall be drawn from the Club Account except by cheque signed by two of the three designated signatories. All monies payable to the club shall be received by the treasurer and deposited in the Club Account.

b   The income and assets of the club (the club property) shall be applied only in furtherance of the objects of the club.

c   The club committee shall have power to authorize the payment of remuneration and expenses to any member of the club and to any other person or persons for services rendered to the club.

d   The club shall prepare an annual financial statement in such form as shall be published by The Football Association from time to time.

e   The club property, other than the Club Account, shall be vested in not less than two and no more than four custodians (the Custodians), one of whom shall be the treasurer. The Custodians shall deal with the club property as directed by decisions of the club committee and entry in the minute book shall be conclusive evidence of such a decision.

f   The Custodians shall be appointed by the club in a General Meeting and shall hold office until death or resignation unless removed by a resolution passed at a General Meeting.

g   On their removal or resignation, a Custodian shall execute a Conveyance, in such form as is published by The Football Association from time to time, to a newly-elected Custodian or the existing Custodians as directed by the club committee. On the death of a Custodian, any club property vested in them shall be vested automatically in the surviving Custodians. If there is only one surviving Custodian, a Special General Meeting shall be convened as soon as possible to appoint another Custodian.

h   The Custodians shall be entitled to an indemnity out of the club property for all expenses and other liabilities reasonably incurred by them in carrying out their duties.

Dissolution

a   A resolution to dissolve the club shall only be proposed at a General Meeting and shall be carried by a majority of at least three-quarters of the members present.

b   The dissolution shall take effect from the date of the resolution and the members of the club committee shall be responsible for the winding up of the assets and liabilities of the club.

LEARNING

Appendix 2: Example of an anti-discrimination policy

- _____ Football Club is responsible for setting standards and values to apply throughout the club at every level. Football belongs to, and should be enjoyed by, everyone equally. Our commitment is to eliminate discrimination whether by reason of gender, sexual orientation, race, nationality, ethnic origin, colour, religion or disability.

- Equality of opportunity at _____ Football Club means that in all our activities we will not discriminate or in any way treat anyone less favourably on grounds of sex, sexual orientation, race, nationality, ethnic origin, colour, religion or disability.

  This includes:

  - The advertisement for volunteers.
  - The selection of candidates for volunteers.
  - Courses.
  - External coaching, and education activities and awards.
  - Football development activities.
  - Selection for teams.
  - Appointments to honorary positions.

- _____ Football Club will not tolerate sexual or racially-based harassment or other discriminatory behaviour, whether physical or verbal and will work to ensure that such behaviour is met with appropriate action in whatever context it occurs.

- _____ Football Club is committed to the development of the programme of ongoing training and awareness-raising events and activities in order to promote the eradication of discrimination within its own organization and in the wider context, within football as a whole.

Appendix 3: Example of an equal opportunities policy

- _____ Football Club is committed to a policy of equal treatment of all members and requires all members of whatever level or authority, to abide and adhere to this general principle and the requirements of the Codes of Practice issued by the Equal Opportunities Commission and Commission for Racial Equality.

- All members are expected to abide by the requirements of the Race Relations Act 1976, Sex Discrimination Act 1986 and Disability Discrimination Act 1995. Specifically, discrimination is prohibited in:

  - Treating any individual on grounds of gender, colour, marital status, race, nationality or ethnic or national origin, religion, sexual orientation or disability less favourably than others.

  - Expecting an individual solely on the grounds stated above to comply with requirement(s) for any reason whatsoever related to their membership, which are different to the requirements for others.

  - Imposing on an individual requirements which are in effect more onerous on that individual than they are on any other.

For example, this would include applying a condition (which is not warranted by the requirements of the position) which makes it more difficult for members of a particular race or sex to comply than others not of that race or sex.

- Victimization of an individual.

- Harassment of an individual (which for the purposes of this policy and the actions and sanction applicable thereto is regarded as discrimination).

- Any other act or omission of an act, which has as its effect the disadvantaging of a member against another, or others, purely on the above grounds. Thus, in all the club's recruitment, selection, promotion and training processes, as well as disciplinary and other matters (in other words all instances where those in control of members are required to make judgements between them) it is essential that merit, experience, skills and temperament are considered as objectively as possible.

- _____ Football Club commits itself to the immediate investigation of any claims of discrimination on the above grounds and where such is found to be the case, a requirement that the practice cease forthwith, restitution of damage or loss (if necessary) and to the investigation of any member accused of discrimination.

- Any member found guilty of discrimination will be instructed to desist forthwith. Since discrimination in its many forms is against the Football Club's policy, any members offending will be dealt with under the disciplinary procedure.

- _____ Football Club commits itself to the person with disabilities whenever possible and will treat such members, in aspects of their recruitment and membership, in exactly the same manner as other members. The difficulties of their disablement permitting, assistance will be given wherever possible to ensure that members with disabilities are helped in gaining access. Appropriate training will be made to such members who request it.

LEARNING

Appendix 4: Example of membership registration form/parental consent

Full name: _____

Home address: _____

Postcode: _____

Home telephone no.: _____ Date of birth: _____

Ethnic origin (Please tick):   White   ☐
                                        Chinese   ☐
                                         Black African ☐
                                         Black Caribbean ☐
                                         Black other   ☐
                                         Pakistani   ☐
                                         Indian   ☐
                                         Other (please specify) _____

Player position (If applying as a playing member) (Please tick)
Goalkeeper ☐   Defender ☐   Mid-field ☐   Forward ☐

Non-playing skills
Coach ☐   Administrator ☐   Fund-raising ☐   Other ☐

Education details (if applicable)

Headteacher: _____

Physical education/teacher: _____

School: _____

Address: _____

County: _____

Postcode: _____

Current school year: _____

Telephone no.: _____ (District/code) _____

Medical details

Please indicate if you have any medical conditions we should be
aware of (e.g. asthma).

_____

_____

_____

Emergency parent/carer details

Status (Please tick):   Mr ☐   Mrs ☐   Ms   Other _____

First name: _____

Surname: _____

Emergency telephone no.: _____

Mobile no.: _____

In the event that the above named person cannot be reached,
please give two extra emergency contact names and numbers:

Name: _____ Emergency contact no.: _____

Name: _____ Emergency contact no.: _____

Parental consent

In the event that my son/daughter is injured while playing football/travelling to and from football events and I cannot be contacted on the above number, I hereby give my consent for my child to receive medical attention.

Signed: _____ Date: _____

Print name: _____

I agree to be bound by and to observe the club rules and the Rules and Regulations of The Football Association Limited and Football Association, and all competitions in which the club participates.

I enclose £ _____ as a membership fee to be repayable if this application is not successful.

I consent to disclosure by County Football Association.

Signature: _____

LEARNING

Appendix 5: Child protection and Best Practice

The Football Association launched the biggest and most wide-ranging sports Child Protection programme in the world in 2000, aiming to tackle head-on everything from serious sexual abuse to swearing. A specific Child Protection Department within The FA was set up to deal with all allegations of abuse of children in football and an FA/NSPCC (National Society for the Prevention of Cruelty to Children) child protection helpline (Tel: 0808 800 5000) was established.

At the same time, an educational team was set to work on how to teach adults in the game about how they should work with children, and what they should do if they come across unacceptable behaviour in others. Since then, over 60,000 people have been trained through the three-hour 'Child Protection and Best Practice' workshop devised by the education teams. Thus, there are 60,000 extra pairs of eyes who know more about looking after children than they did before they went on the workshop and who now know what to do if they notice something that concerns them.

Many more will benefit from the interactive pack *Child Protection and Best Practice – A Guide,* which is designed for anyone involved with children's football. This is available on CD-ROM or video and is easy to follow. The pack is designed to be worked through at home, and it provides awareness of best practice in child protection. There is also a network of trained Child Protection officers at every County FA, and a growing network of Designated Persons in leagues and clubs. A process of vetting has also begun, whereby every single person who works with children in football (and eventually every coach, referee, player and medic registered with the FA) will have a criminal record check.

For further information on The FA's *Child Protection and Best Practice* programme, contact The FA (Tel: 0207 745 4909; E-mail: goal@TheFA.com.

Appendix 6: Code of Conduct

Football is the national game. All those involved with the game at every level and whether as a player, match official, coach, owner or administrator, have a responsibility, above and beyond compliance with the law, to act according to the highest standards of integrity, and to ensure that the reputation of the game is, and remains, high. This code applies to all those involved in football under the auspices of The Football Association.

Community

Football, at all levels, is a vital part of a community. Football will take into account community feeling when making decisions.

Equality

Football is opposed to discrimination of any form and will promote measures to prevent it, in whatever form, from being expressed.

Participants

Football recognizes the sense of ownership felt by those who participate at all levels of the game. This includes those who play, those who coach or help in any way, and those who officiate, as well as administrators and supporters. Football is committed to appropriate consultation.

Young people

Football acknowledges the extent of its influence over young people and pledges to set a positive example.

Propriety

Football acknowledges that public confidence demands the highest standards of financial and administrative behavioiur within the game, and will not tolerate corruption or improper practices.

Trust and respect

Football will uphold a relationship of trust and respect between all involved in the game, whether they are individuals, clubs or other organizations.

Violence

Football rejects the use of violence of any nature by anyone involved in the game.

Fairness

Football is committed to fairness in its dealings with all involved in the game.

Integrity and fair play

Football is committed to the principle of playing to win, consistent with fair play.

Code of Conduct for coaches

Coaches are key to the establishment of ethics within football. Their concept of ethics and their attitude directly affects the behaviour of players under their supervision. Coaches are, therefore, expected to pay particular care to the moral aspect of their conduct.

Coaches have to be aware that almost all of their everyday decisions and choices of actions, as well as strategic targets, have ethical implications.

It is natural that winning constitutes a basic concern for coaches. This code is not intended to conflict with that. However, the code calls for coaches to disassociate themselves from a 'win-at-all-costs' attitude.

Increased responsibility is requested from coaches involved in coaching young people. The health, safety, welfare and moral education of young people are the first priority, before the achievement of the reputation of the club, school, coach or parent.

Set out below is the FA Coaches' Association Code of Conduct (which reflects the standards expressed by the National Coaching Foundation and the National Association of Sports Coaches), which forms the benchmark for all involved in coaching.

1 Coaches must respect the rights, dignity and worth of each and every person and treat each equally within the context of the sport.

2 Coaches must place the well-being and safety of each player above all other considerations, including the development of performance.

3 Coaches must adhere to all guidelines laid down by governing bodies.

4 Coaches must develop an appropriate working relationship with each player based on mutual trust and respect.

5 Coaches must not exert undue influence to obtain personal benefit or reward.

6 Coaches must encourage and guide players to accept responsibility for their own behaviour and performance.

7 Coaches must ensure that the activities they direct or advocate are appropriate for the age, maturity, experience and ability of players.

8 Coaches should, at the outset, clarify with the players (and, where appropriate, parent) exactly what is expected of them and also what they are entitled to expect from their coach.

9 Coaches must co-operate fully with other specialists (e.g. other coaches, officials, sports scientists, doctors, physiotherapists) in the best interests of the player.

10 Coaches must always promote the positive aspects of the sport (e.g. fair play) and never condone violations of the Laws of the Game, behaviour contrary to the spirit of the Laws of the Game or relevant rules and regulations or the use of prohibited substances or techniques.

11 Coaches must consistently display high standards of behaviour and appearance.

12 Not to use or tolerate inappropriate language.

Code of Conduct for players

Players are the most important people in the sport. Playing for the team, and for the team to win, is the most fundamental part of the game. But winning at any cost is not the idea – fair play and respect for all others in the game is fundamentally important.

This Code is focused on players involved in top-class football. Nevertheless, the key concepts in the Code are valid for players at all levels.

Obligations towards the game

A player should:

1 Make every effort to develop their own sporting abilities, in terms of skill, technique, tactics and stamina.

2 Give maximum effort and strive for the best possible performance during a game, even if his/her team is in a psoition where the desired result has already been achieved.

3 Set a positive example for others, particularly young players and supporters.

4   Avoid all forms of gamesmanship and time-wasting.

5   Always have regard to the best interests of the game, including where publicly expressing an opinion on the game and any particular aspect of it, including others involved in the game.

6   Not use inappropriate language.

Obligations towards one's own team

A player should:

1   Make every effort consistent with fair play and the Laws of the Game to help his/her own team win.

2   Resist any influence which might, or might be seen to, bring into question his/her commitment to the team winning.

Respect for the Laws of the Game and competition rules

A player should:

1   Know and abide by the Laws, rules and spirit of the game, and the competition rules.

2   Accept success and failure, victory and defeat, equally.

3   Resist any temptation to take banned substances or use banned techniques.

Respect towards opponents

A player should:

1   Treat opponents with due respect at all times, irrespective of the result of the game.

2   Safeguard the physical fitness of opponents, avoid violence and rough play, and help injured opponents.

Respect towards the match officials

A player should:

1   Accept the decision of the match official without protest.

2   Avoid words or actions which may mislead a match official.

3   Show due respect towards match officials.

Respect towards team officials

A player should:

1 Abide by the instructions of their coach and team officials, provided they do not contradict the spirit of this Code.

2 Show due respect towards the team officials of the opposition.

Obligations towards the supporters

A player should:

1 Show due respect to the interests of the supporters.

Code of Conduct for team officials

This Code applies to all team/club officials (although some items may not apply to all officials).

Obligations towards the game

The team official should:

1 Set a positive example for others, particularly young players and supporters.

2 Promote and develop his/her own team having regard for the interest of the players, supporters and reputation of the national game.

3 Share knowledge and experience when invited to do so, taking into account the interest of the body that has requested this rather than personal interests.

4 Avoid all forms of gamesmanship.

5 Show due respect to match officials and others involved in the game.

6 Always have regard for the best interests of the game, including where publicly expressing an opinion of the game and any particular aspect of it, including others involved in the game.

7 Not use or tolerate inappropriate language.

Obligations towards the team

The Team Official should:

1 Make every effort to develop the sporting, technical and tactical levels of the club/team, and to obtain the best results by the team, using all permitted means.

2 Give priority to the interests of the team over individual interests.

3 Resist all illegal or unsporting influences, including banned substances and techniques.

4 Promote ethical principles.

5 Show due respect to the interests of players, coaches and other officials, at their own club/team and others.

Obligations towards the supporters

The Team Offical should:

1 Show due respect to the interests of supporters.

Respect towards the Match Officials

The Team Official should:

1 Accept the decisions of the Match Official without protest.

2 Avoid words or actions which may mislead a Match Official.

3 Show due respect towards Match Officials.

Code of Conduct for parents/spectators

Parents and spectators have a great influence on children's enjoyment and success in football. All children play football because they first and foremost love the game – it's fun. Remember that however good a child becomes at football within your club, it is important to reinforce the message to parents/spectators that positive encouragement will contribute to:

• Children enjoying football.

• A sense of personal achievement.

- Self-esteem.
- Helping to improve the child's skill and techniques.

A parent's/spectator's expectations and attitudes have a significant bearing on a child's attitude towards:

- Other players.
- Officials.
- Managers.
- Spectators.

Ensure that parents/spectators within your club are always positive and show encouragement towards all of the children, not just their own.

Encourage parents/spectators to:

- **Applaud the opposition as well as your own team.**
- **Avoid coaching the child during the game.**
- **Avoid shouting and screaming.**
- **Respect the referee's decision.**
- **Give attention to each of the children involved in football, not just the most talented.**
- **Give encouragement to everyone to participate in football.**

Ensure that the parents/spectators within your club agree and adhere to your club's Code of Conduct and Child Protection policy.

Contacts

Fédération Internationale de Football Association (FIFA)
FIFA House
Hitzigweg 11
PO Box 85
8030 Zurich
Switzerland
Tel: +41-43/222 7777
Fax: +41-43/222 7878
Internet: http://www.fifa.com

Confederations

Asian Football Confederation (AFC)
AFC House, Jalan 1/155B
Bukit Jalil
Kuala Lumpur 57000
Malaysia
Tel: +60-3/8994 3388
Fax: +60-3/8994 2689
Internet: http://www.footballasia.com

Confédération Africaine de Football (CAF)
3 Abdel Khalek Sarwat Street
El Hay El Motamayez
PO Box 23
6th October City
Egypt
Tel: +20-2/837 1000
Fax: +20-2/837 0006
Internet: http://www.cafonline.com

Confederation of North, Central American and Caribbean Association Football (CONCACAF)
Central American and Caribbean Association Football
725 Fifth Avenue, 17th Floor
New York, NY 10022
USA
Tel: +1-212/308 0044
Fax: +1-212/308 1851
Internet: http://www.concacaf.net

Confederación Sudamericana de Fútbol (CONMEBOL)
Autopista Aeropuerto Internacional y
Leonismo Luqueño
Luque (Gran Asunción)
Paraguay
Tel: +595-21/645 781
Fax: +595-21/645 791
Internet: http://www.conmebol.com

Oceania Football Confederation (OFC)
Ericsson Stadium
12 Maurice Road
PO Box 62 586
Penrose
Auckland
New Zealand
Tel: +64-9/525 8161
Fax: +64-9/525 8164
Internet: http://www.oceaniafootball
.com

Union European Football Association (UEFA)
Route de Genève 46
Nyon 1260
Switzerland
Tel: +41-22/994 4444
Fax: +41-22/994 4488
Internet: http://www.uefa.com

Associations

Argentina
Asociación del Fútbol Argentino (AFA)
Viamonte 1366/76
Buenos Aires 1053
Tel: ++54-11/4372 7900
Fax: ++54-11/4375 4410
Internet: http://www.afa.org.ar

Australia
Soccer Australia Limited (ASF)
Level 3
East Stand, Stadium Australia
Edwin Flack Avenue
Homebush NSW 2127
Tel: ++61-2/9739 5555
Fax: ++61-2/9739 5590
Internet: http://www.socceraustralia
.com.au

Belgium
Union Royale Belge des Sociétés de Football Assocation (URBSFA/KBV)
145 Avenue Houba de Strooper
Bruxelles 1020
Tel: ++32-2/477 1211
Fax: ++32-2/478 2391
Internet: http://www.footbel.com

Brazil
Confederação Brasileira de Futebol (CBF)
Rua Victor Civita 66
Bloco 1 – Edifício 5 – 5 Andar
Barra da Tijuca
Rio de Janeiro 22775-040
Tel: ++55-21/3870 3610
Fax: ++55-21/3870 3612
Internet: http://www.cbfnews.com

Cameroon
Fédération Camerounaise de Football (FECAFOOT)
Case postale 1116
Yaoundé
Tel: ++237/221 0012
Fax: ++237/221 6662
Internet: http://www.cameroon.fifa.com

ción Española de
EF)
al, s/n
ostale 385
30
1/495 9800
91/495 9801
ttp://www.rfef.es

en
Fotbollförbundet (SVFF)
216
123
6-8/735 0900
46-8/735 0901
: http://www.svenskfotboll.se

zerland
eizerischer Fussball-Verband
/ASF)
ach
15 3000
+41-31/950 8111
++41-31/950 8181
rnet: http://www.football.ch

unisia
édération Tunisienne de Football
TF)
aison des Fédérations Sportives
Cité Olympique
Tunis 1003
Tel: ++216-71/233 303
Fax: ++216-71/767 929
Internet: http://www.ftf.org.tn

Turkey

Türkiye Futbol Federasyonu (TFF)
Konaklar Mah. Ihlamurlu Sok. 9
4. Levent
Istanbul 80620
Tel: ++90-212/282 7020
Fax: ++90-212/282 7015
Internet: http://www.tff.org

United States of America

US Soccer Federation (USSF)
US Soccer House
1801 S. Prairie Avenue
Chicago IL 60616
Tel: ++1-312/808 1300
Fax: ++1-312/808 1301
Internet: http://www.ussoccer.com

Uruguay

**Asociación Uruguaya de Fútbol
(AUF)**
Guayabo 1531
Montevideo 11200
Tel: ++59-82/400 4814
Fax: ++59-82/409 0550
Internet: http://www.auf.org.uy

Wales

**The Football Association of Wales,
Ltd (FAW)**
Plymouth Chambers
3 Westgate Street
Cardiff CF10 1DP
Tel: ++44-29/2037 2325
Fax: ++44-29/2034 3961
Internet: http://www.faw.org.uk

For details of County FAs please see **www.TheFA.com**/Grassroots

Canada

**The Canadian Soccer Association
(CSA)**
Place Soccer Canada
237 Metcalfe Street
Ottawa ONT K2P 1R2
Tel: ++1-613/237 7678
Fax: ++1-613/237 1516
Internet: http://www.canadasoccer.com

Costa Rica

**Federación Costarricense de
Fútbol (FEDEFUTBOL)**
Costado Norte Estatua León Cortés
San José 670-1000
Tel: ++506/222 1544
Fax: ++506/255 2674
Internet: http://www.fedefutbol.com

Croatia

Croatian Football Federation (HNS)
Rusanova 13
Zagreb 10 000
Tel: ++385-1/236 1555
Fax: ++385-1/244 1501
Internet: http://www.hns-cff.hr

Czech Republic

**Football Association of Czech
Republic (CMFS)**
Diskarska 100
Praha 6 16017
Tel: ++420-2/3302 9111
Fax: ++420-2/3335 3107
Internet: http://www.fotbal.cz

Denmark

**Danish Football Association
(DBU)**
Idrættens Hus
Brøndby Stadion 20
Brøndby 2605
Tel: ++45-43/262 222
Fax: ++45-43/262 245
Internet: http://www.dbu.dk

England

The Football Association (The FA)
25 Soho Square
London W1D 4FA
Tel: ++44-207/745 4545
Fax: ++44-207/745 4546
Internet: http://www.TheFA.com

Finland

Suomen Palloliitto (SPL/FBF)
Urheilukatu 5
PO Box 191
Helsinki 00251
Tel: ++358-9/7421 51
Fax: ++358-9/7421 5200
Internet: http://www.palloliitto.fi

France

**Fédération Française de Football
(FFF)**
60 Bis Avenue d'Iéna
Paris 75116
Tel: ++33-1/4431 7300
Fax: ++33-1/4720 8296
Internet: http://www.fff.fr

Germany

Deutscher Fussball-Bund (DFB)
Otto-Fleck-Schneise 6
Postfach 71 02 65
Frankfurt Am Main 60492
Tel: ++49-69/678 80
Fax: ++49-69/678 8266
Internet: http://www.dfb.de

Greece

Hellenic Football Federation (HFF)
137 Singrou Avenue
Nea Smirni
Athens 17121
Tel: ++30-210/930 6000
Fax: ++30-210/935 9666
Internet: http://www.epo.gr

Ireland Republic

**The Football Association of
Ireland (FAI)**

80 Merrion Square, South
Dublin 2
Tel: ++353-1/676 6864
Fax: ++353-1/661 0931
Internet: http://www.fai.ie

Italy

**Federazione Italiana Giuoco Calcio
(FIGC)**

Via Gregorio Allegri, 14
Roma 00198
Tel: ++39-06/84 911
Fax: ++39-06/84 912 526
Internet: http://www.figc.it

Japan

Japan Football Association (JFA)

JFA House
3-10-15, Hongo
Bunkyo-ku
Tokyo 113-0033
Tel: ++81-3/3830 2004
Fax: ++81-3/3830 2005
Internet: http://www.jfa.or.jp

Kenya

Kenya Football Federation (KFF)

PO Box 40234
Nairobi
Tel: ++254-2/608 422
Fax: ++254-2/249 855
Email: kff@todays.co.ke

Korea Republic

Korea Football Association (KFA)

1-131 Sinmunno, 2-ga
Jongno-Gu
Seoul 110-062
Tel: ++82-2/733 6764
Fax: ++82-2/735 2755
Internet: http://www.kfa.or.kr

Mexico

**Federación Mexicana de Fútbol
Asociación, A.C. (FMF)**

Colima No. 373
Colonia Roma
Mexico, D.F. 06700
Tel: ++52-55/5241 0190
Fax: ++52-55/5241 0191
Internet: http://www.femexfut.org.mx

Netherlands

**Koninklijke Nederlandse
Voetbalbond (KNVB)**

Woudenbergseweg 56–58
PO Box 515
Am Zeist 3700 AM
Tel: ++31-343/499 201
Fax: ++31-343/499 189
Internet: http://www.knvb.nl

Nigeria

Nigeria Football Association (NFA)

Plot 2033, Olusegun
Obasanjo Way, Zone 7, Wuse Abuja
PO Box 5101 Garki
Abuja
Tel: ++234-9/523 7326
Fax: ++234-9/523 7327
Email: nfa@microaccess.com

Northern Ireland

**Irish Football Association Ltd.
(IFA)**

20 Windsor Avenue
Belfast BT9 6EE
Tel: ++44-28/9066 9458
Fax: ++44-28/9066 7620
Internet: http://www.irishfa.com

Paraguay

**Asociación Paraguaya de Fútbol
(APF)**

Estadio de los Defensores del Chaco
Calle Mayor Martinez 1393
Asunción
Tel: ++595-21/480 120
Fax: ++595-21/480 124
Internet: http://www.apf.org.py

Poland

Polish Football Association (PZPN)

Polski Zwiazek Pilki Noznej
Miodowa 1
Warsaw 00-080
Tel: ++48-22/827 0914
Fax: ++48-22/827 0704
Internet: http://www.pzpn.pl

Portugal

**Federação Portuguesa de Futebol
(FPF)**

Praça de Alegria, N. 25
PO Box 21.100
Lisbon 1250-004
Tel: ++351-21/325 2700
Fax: ++351-21/325 2780
Internet: http://www.fpf.pt

Ro

**Rom
(FRF)**
House
Str. Ser
Buchare
Tel: ++40
Fax: ++40
Internet: h

Russia

Football Un
8 Luzhnetskay
Moscow 119 9
Tel: ++7-095/2(
Fax: ++7-502/22
Internet: http://

Scotland

**The Scottish Foo
(SFA)**
Hampden Park
Glasgow G42 9AY
Tel: ++44-141/616 60(
Fax: ++44-141/616 600
Internet: http://www.sc

South Africa

**South African Football
Association (SAFA)**
First National Bank Stadium
PO Box 910
Johannesburg 2000
Tel: ++27-11/494 3522
Fax: ++27-11/494 3013
Internet: http://www.safa.net

Spain

**Real Feder
Fútbol (RF**
Ramon y Ca
Apartado p
Madrid 28
Tel: ++34-9
Fax: ++34-
Internet: h

Swede

Svenska
PO Box
Solna 17
Tel: ++4
Fax: ++
Interne

Swit

**Schw
(SFV**
Postf
Berr
Tel:
Fax
Int

LEARNING

Index

All about FA Learning

FA Learning is the Educational Division of The FA and is responsible for the delivery, co-ordination and promotion of its extensive range of educational products and services. This includes all courses and resources for coaching, refereeing, psychology, sports science, medical exercise, child protection, crowd safety and teacher training.

The diverse interests of those involved in football ensures that FA Learning remains committed to providing resources and activities suitable for all individuals whatever their interests, experience or level of expertise.

Whether you're a Premier League Manager, sports psychologist or interested parent, our aim is to have courses and resources available that will improve your knowledge and understanding.

If you've enjoyed reading this book and found the content useful then why not take a look at FA Learning's website to find out the types of courses and additional resources available to help you continue your football development.

The website contains information on all the national courses and events managed by The FA as well as information on a number of online resources:

- **Psychology for Soccer Level 1 – Our first online qualification.**
- **Soccer Star – Free online coaching tool for young players.**
- **Soccer Parent – Free online course for parents.**

All these resources can be accessed at home from your own PC and are currently used by thousands of people across the world.

Psychology for Soccer Level 1

Enrol today and join hundreds of others around the world taking part in FA Learning's first ever online qualification.

This pioneering project is the first of its kind to be provided by any Football Governing Body and is available to anyone with access to the internet. There are no additional qualifications required to take part other than an interest in learning more about the needs of young players and an email address!

The course is aimed at coaches, parents and teachers of 7–12 year olds looking to gain an introduction to psychology and features modules based on 'true to life' player, coach and parent scenarios.

Psychology for Soccer Level 1 is a completely interactive, multimedia learning experience. Don't just take our word for it, read some of the comments from those that have already completed the course:

'Wow what a wonderful course! Thank you for the time and effort to make this possible.' **Tracy Scott**

'Just passed the final assessment ... it was a good experience to learn this way and hopefully more qualifications will become available in this format. Thanks.' **Shayne Hall**

'I am a professional football coach working in schools and clubs and have travelled all around the world. I have really enjoyed the literature in this course and it has made me think about how I should address my coaching sessions. I want to progress in the field of sport psychology and this course has whetted my appetite for this subject.' **Chris Rafael Sabater**

The course modules are:

- Psychology and Soccer
- Motivation
- Learning and Acquiring skills
- Psychological Development
- Environment and Social Influences

In addition to the five course modules, learners also have access to a number of further benefits included as part of the course fee. The benefits include:

- **Three months support from qualified FA tutors**
- **Classroom specific online discussion forums**
- **A global online discussion forum**
- **All successful students receive a FA Qualification in psychology**
- **An exclusive resource area containing over 100 articles and web links relating to coaching 7–12 year olds.**

Within the five modules, there are over 20 sessions totaling over eight hours worth of content. Including the use of discussion forums, resource area and the course tasks, we anticipate the course will take on average 20 hours to complete.

For more information and to enroll on the course visit
www.**TheFA.com**/FALearning.

THE OFFICIAL FA GUIDE TO
PSYCHOLOGY FOR FOOTBALL

Be a part of the game

The Official FA Guide to Psychology for Football is an introductory guide for anyone who wants to understand the needs of young players.

This book includes:
- **understanding the motivation, learning and development of players**
- **the affect of a player's environment**
- **how to develop individual strategies.**

Packed with practical exercises, information and expert advice, this book will improve your understanding and enhance your ability and enjoyment of the world's greatest game.

The author, **Dr Andy Cale**, is The Football Association's Education Advisor and was previously a lecturer in Sports Psychology at Loughborough University.

FA Learning
'learning through football'

TheFA.com/FALearning

Visit the website for information on all FA Learning's educational activities.

LEARNING

Canada

The Canadian Soccer Association (CSA)
Place Soccer Canada
237 Metcalfe Street
Ottawa ONT K2P 1R2
Tel: ++1-613/237 7678
Fax: ++1-613/237 1516
Internet: http://www.canadasoccer.com

Costa Rica

Federación Costarricense de Fútbol (FEDEFUTBOL)
Costado Norte Estatua León Cortés
San José 670-1000
Tel: ++506/222 1544
Fax: ++506/255 2674
Internet: http://www.fedefutbol.com

Croatia

Croatian Football Federation (HNS)
Rusanova 13
Zagreb 10 000
Tel: ++385-1/236 1555
Fax: ++385-1/244 1501
Internet: http://www.hns-cff.hr

Czech Republic

Football Association of Czech Republic (CMFS)
Diskarska 100
Praha 6 16017
Tel: ++420-2/3302 9111
Fax: ++420-2/3335 3107
Internet: http://www.fotbal.cz

Denmark

Danish Football Association (DBU)
Idrættens Hus
Brøndby Stadion 20
Brøndby 2605
Tel: ++45-43/262 222
Fax: ++45-43/262 245
Internet: http://www.dbu.dk

England

The Football Association (The FA)
25 Soho Square
London W1D 4FA
Tel: ++44-207/745 4545
Fax: ++44-207/745 4546
Internet: http://www.TheFA.com

Finland

Suomen Palloliitto (SPL/FBF)
Urheilukatu 5
PO Box 191
Helsinki 00251
Tel: ++358-9/7421 51
Fax: ++358-9/7421 5200
Internet: http://www.palloliitto.fi

France

Fédération Française de Football (FFF)
60 Bis Avenue d'Iéna
Paris 75116
Tel: ++33-1/4431 7300
Fax: ++33-1/4720 8296
Internet: http://www.fff.fr

Germany

Deutscher Fussball-Bund (DFB)
Otto-Fleck-Schneise 6
Postfach 71 02 65
Frankfurt Am Main 60492
Tel: ++49-69/678 80
Fax: ++49-69/678 8266
Internet: http://www.dfb.de

Greece

Hellenic Football Federation (HFF)
137 Singrou Avenue
Nea Smirni
Athens 17121
Tel: ++30-210/930 6000
Fax: ++30-210/935 9666
Internet: http://www.epo.gr

Ireland Republic
The Football Association of Ireland (FAI)
80 Merrion Square, South
Dublin 2
Tel: ++353-1/676 6864
Fax: ++353-1/661 0931
Internet: http://www.fai.ie

Italy
Federazione Italiana Giuoco Calcio (FIGC)
Via Gregorio Allegri, 14
Roma 00198
Tel: ++39-06/84 911
Fax: ++39-06/84 912 526
Internet: http://www.figc.it

Japan
Japan Football Association (JFA)
JFA House
3-10-15, Hongo
Bunkyo-ku
Tokyo 113-0033
Tel: ++81-3/3830 2004
Fax: ++81-3/3830 2005
Internet: http://www.jfa.or.jp

Kenya
Kenya Football Federation (KFF)
PO Box 40234
Nairobi
Tel: ++254-2/608 422
Fax: ++254-2/249 855
Email: kff@todays.co.ke

Korea Republic
Korea Football Association (KFA)
1-131 Sinmunno, 2-ga
Jongno-Gu
Seoul 110-062
Tel: ++82-2/733 6764
Fax: ++82-2/735 2755
Internet: http://www.kfa.or.kr

Mexico
Federación Mexicana de Fútbol Asociación, A.C. (FMF)
Colima No. 373
Colonia Roma
Mexico, D.F. 06700
Tel: ++52-55/5241 0190
Fax: ++52-55/5241 0191
Internet: http://www.femexfut.org.mx

Netherlands
Koninklijke Nederlandse Voetbalbond (KNVB)
Woudenbergseweg 56–58
PO Box 515
Am Zeist 3700 AM
Tel: ++31-343/499 201
Fax: ++31-343/499 189
Internet: http://www.knvb.nl

Nigeria
Nigeria Football Association (NFA)
Plot 2033, Olusegun
Obasanjo Way, Zone 7, Wuse Abuja
PO Box 5101 Garki
Abuja
Tel: ++234-9/523 7326
Fax: ++234-9/523 7327
Email: nfa@microaccess.com

Northern Ireland
Irish Football Association Ltd. (IFA)
20 Windsor Avenue
Belfast BT9 6EE
Tel: ++44-28/9066 9458
Fax: ++44-28/9066 7620
Internet: http://www.irishfa.com

Paraguay
Asociación Paraguaya de Fútbol (APF)
Estadio de los Defensores del Chaco
Calle Mayor Martinez 1393
Asunción
Tel: ++595-21/480 120
Fax: ++595-21/480 124
Internet: http://www.apf.org.py

Poland
Polish Football Association (PZPN)
Polski Zwiazek Pilki Noznej
Miodowa 1
Warsaw 00-080
Tel: ++48-22/827 0914
Fax: ++48-22/827 0704
Internet: http://www.pzpn.pl

Portugal
Federação Portuguesa de Futebol (FPF)
Praça de Alegria, N. 25
PO Box 21.100
Lisbon 1250-004
Tel: ++351-21/325 2700
Fax: ++351-21/325 2780
Internet: http://www.fpf.pt

Romania
Romanian Football Federation (FRF)
House of Football
Str. Serg. Serbanica Vasile 12
Bucharest 73412
Tel: ++40-21/325 0678
Fax: ++40-21/325 0679
Internet: http://www.frf.ro

Russia
Football Union of Russia (RFU)
8 Luzhnetskaya Naberezhnaja
Moscow 119 992
Tel: ++7-095/201 1637
Fax: ++7-502/220 2037
Internet: http://www.rfs.ru

Scotland
The Scottish Football Association (SFA)
Hampden Park
Glasgow G42 9AY
Tel: ++44-141/616 6000
Fax: ++44-141/616 6001
Internet: http://www.scottishfa.co.uk

South Africa
South African Football Association (SAFA)
First National Bank Stadium
PO Box 910
Johannesburg 2000
Tel: ++27-11/494 3522
Fax: ++27-11/494 3013
Internet: http://www.safa.net

Spain
Real Federación Española de Fútbol (RFEF)
Ramon y Cajal, s/n
Apartado postale 385
Madrid 28230
Tel: ++34-91/495 9800
Fax: ++34-91/495 9801
Internet: http://www.rfef.es

Sweden
Svenska Fotbollförbundet (SVFF)
PO Box 1216
Solna 17 123
Tel: ++46-8/735 0900
Fax: ++46-8/735 0901
Internet: http://www.svenskfotboll.se

Switzerland
Schweizerischer Fussball-Verband (SFV/ASF)
Postfach
Bern 15 3000
Tel: ++41-31/950 8111
Fax: ++41-31/950 8181
Internet: http://www.football.ch

Tunisia
Fédération Tunisienne de Football (FTF)
Maison des Fédérations Sportives
Cité Olympique
Tunis 1003
Tel: ++216-71/233 303
Fax: ++216-71/767 929
Internet: http://www.ftf.org.tn

Turkey
Türkiye Futbol Federasyonu (TFF)
Konaklar Mah. Ihlamurlu Sok. 9
4. Levent
Istanbul 80620
Tel: ++90-212/282 7020
Fax: ++90-212/282 7015
Internet: http://www.tff.org

United States of America
US Soccer Federation (USSF)
US Soccer House
1801 S. Prairie Avenue
Chicago IL 60616
Tel: ++1-312/808 1300
Fax: ++1-312/808 1301
Internet: http://www.ussoccer.com

Uruguay
Asociación Uruguaya de Fútbol (AUF)
Guayabo 1531
Montevideo 11200
Tel: ++59-82/400 4814
Fax: ++59-82/409 0550
Internet: http://www.auf.org.uy

Wales
The Football Association of Wales, Ltd (FAW)
Plymouth Chambers
3 Westgate Street
Cardiff CF10 1DP
Tel: ++44-29/2037 2325
Fax: ++44-29/2034 3961
Internet: http://www.faw.org.uk

For details of County FAs please see **www.TheFA.com**/Grassroots